Marguerite Patten

Cooking for the Family
in color

edited by
Helen Feingold

LONGMEADOW
PRESS

Introduction

If you enjoy cooking, it is doubly satisfying to see family and friends enjoy the dishes you have prepared.

There are occasions, of course, when shopping and cooking seem very time-consuming and tiresome tasks, but that might be the time to take a new look at your menus and decide to experiment with new ideas. This will provide a challenge, it may well save money and the family will appreciate a new look to their meals.

It is, of course, very important to provide balanced, varied meals for the family and the recipes in this book have been written with that in mind. Information is provided on proteins, vitamins and minerals to help you make sure that every member of your family is getting the right kind of food. There are also lots of quick tips, budget suggestions and freezing instructions as well as useful hints for making the best possible use of modern kitchen appliances.

This whole book has been planned for family living and it contains a good mixture of economical and special occasion dishes. So start experimenting with your cooking and surprise the family—and, perhaps, yourself.

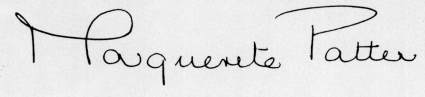

First published in USA 1977 by Longmeadow Press, PO Box 16, Rowayton Station, Norwalk, Connecticut 06853

© 1977 Octopus Books Limited

ISBN 0 7064 0652 4

Produced by Mandarin Publishers Limited, 22a Westlands Road, Quarry Bay, Hong Kong

Printed in Hong Kong

Family Needs

Good food undoubtedly plays a part in keeping all members of the family healthy, from the youngest to the eldest. I am a great believer in family meals being a pleasant "get together", so that they may be enjoyed not only for their food but for the fact that the family can relax; this is why you will find that I have concentrated on family type meals. This does not mean they are all rather plain, for some of the dishes that seem elaborate are very simple to make. I have also given sections, as you will see, on various types of entertaining, for most of us enjoy this.

If your family has varied meals you will undoubtedly be giving them a well balanced diet. It is, however, worthwhile checking now and again to make certain that every member of your family is having the right kind of food.

Proteins
This particular nutrient is found in all meat, poultry, game, in every kind of fish and in cheese, eggs and milk. It is also present in some vegetables such as peas, beans and lentils and in nuts. It is essential to produce strong healthy babies and children and to maintain health throughout our lives. When you allocate money for housekeeping, therefore, this is one of the most important things to consider: is your family having enough protein?

Fats
Some kind of fat is important for producing a feeling of warmth in the body. Butter, margarine and other fats and oils give us this, together with the fat you find on meat and some kinds of fish. Most of us eat too much fat. You need to reduce the amount of fat you eat if you are on a reducing diet as fats are very high in calories.

Carbohydrates
Two kinds of food come under this heading: starch and sugar. Starches are in certain vegetables, such as potatoes, peas and beans, in flour and all the foods that are made with flour, which range from pasta to cookies and cakes; other food such as rice also contains starch.

Sugar is in sugar itself of course and anything made with sugar; jam, cakes, puddings, etc. It is present in honey and syrups.

It is fashionable today to condemn carbohydrates but most of us need a certain amount as they promote energy. If you are on a reducing diet you must cut down, or even cut out, carbohydrates for a time, then quite possibly eat a restricted amount.

Children should not be given too many sweet things as it spoils their appetite for the more important food and can harm their teeth.

Vitamins and Minerals
There are certain vitamins that we all need to keep us well. If you eat a varied diet including fresh foods you will automatically have these; for example, fresh fruit and vegetables give us Vitamin C (ascorbic acid) which is often called the protective vitamin as it builds up resistance to colds and influenza and also helps us to recover after an illness.

In addition to vitamins you will read of the importance of minerals and these also are present in many of our everyday foods. Two of the most important are calcium and iron as calcium keeps teeth and bones healthy and severe lack of iron causes anemia. The best source of calcium is cheese. It is also added to bread, so a meal of bread and cheese is a healthy and enjoyable one. Iron is found in all meat, especially liver, heart and kidneys, and it is also obtained from watercress, spinach, dried apricots and other dried fruit.

As you see, it is not difficult to plan the kinds of meals your family enjoy and at the same time keep an eye upon their nutritional needs.

Modern Kitchen Developments

All around us there are modern developments, but possibly some of the biggest changes have come in our homes, and in no place more than in the kitchen.

The Refrigerator

This is the one place in your home where food is kept at an absolutely safe temperature. Cover food in the refrigerator to prevent inter-mingling of odor, and store food with a strong smell as near the freezing unit as possible. Frozen foods should be stored in the freezing compartment.

The Freezer

There are certain important things to remember when using your freezer.

The food you freeze: a) Check that everything you freeze is really fresh.

b) Although most foods freeze well, there are certain foods that can give problems, e.g. cooked eggs become hard and "rubbery". Sauces, especially if they are creamy, may separate (curdle) during freezing and reheating. I find this is less likely to happen if you use potato flour or cornstarch instead of ordinary flour, see page 54.

I would not choose to freeze mayonnaise, which also has a tendency to separate, but I have frozen left-over dishes containing some mayonnaise with good results.

Lettuce and other salad vegetables lose their crisp texture. Some flavors lose a certain potency in freezing, e.g., garlic and wine. Either make allowance for this or, if possible, add after freezing. Many people feel pastry dishes are better frozen before cooking. In my own home I find it convenient to have both cooked and uncooked pastry dishes.

c) For best results do not keep foods in the freezer longer than the recommended period.

The way to freeze: Follow the manufacturers' recommendations at all times on the care and use of your freezer with special regard to:

a) The part of the freezer in which to place food for rapid freezing and the amount of food to freeze at one time. The faster the food is frozen the better the results.

b) Take the trouble to pack food carefully. Efficient wrapping is important to retain both the fresh flavor and the texture of each food. Tight wrapping and the exclusion of air from packages promotes fast freezing. Certain foods are frozen before wrapping, i.e. decorated cakes etc., but wrap immediately when they are firm. There is a wide choice of packaging materials available: waxed cartons, aluminium foil, thick plastic bags, sheets and containers etc. It may seem expensive to invest in these, but many can be used over again.

c) Keep a record of where the food is stored and the date it is frozen.

After freezing: a) Plan ahead so you allow adequate time to defrost food. Some foods can be cooked from the frozen state. To hasten defrosting stand the wrapped article in cold (not hot) water.

b) Reheat carefully. Allow yourself adequate time to warm the mixture, to prevent burning or curdling.

c) When frozen foods are thawed they become as perishable as fresh foods.

Commercially frozen food

When you have your own freezer or an adequate compartment in a refrigerator you can store commercially frozen foods. Remember these foods have been selected and frozen under ideal conditions and in many cases you will find it better to buy commercially frozen vegetables, for the variety grown has been specially selected for freezing.

Many of the prepared meat and fish dishes are created and cooked by experienced chefs. Follow the recommendations given on the package at all times, for this will ensure your frozen food keeps in perfect condition.

The mixer

Use the whisk and/or beater for creaming, beating and whisking processes. You will find this invaluable, as it saves time and effort.

Use the same techniques for blending mixtures as you would when mixing by hand, i.e. whip cream on a slow speed, do not overbeat; add the eggs gradually to a creamed mixture to avoid curdling. I always fold in the flour by hand when making cakes.

The blender

Use a blender instead of a sieve to make purées of fruit, vegetables, soups. In most cases you will have a perfectly smooth purée, but the blender does not deal with the tiny hard seeds in raspberries and similar fruits. The blender can also be used for making milk shakes and other drinks, stuffings and mayonnaise.

Sometimes you will be advised to add the ingredients gradually, with the motor running. If you try to do this without a cover on the blender you may well have the ingredients splashing out. Some blenders have a removable "cap" in the lid

for this purpose, but if yours does not, the solution is simple. Make a foil cover for the blender with a hole in the center, or make a funnel of foil and fit this into the top of the blender. You can then "feed-in" the ingredients gradually.

Never over-fill the blender, particularly with hot liquids, as the mixture often rises and could force off the lid. It is also wise to start the process of blending on a low speed, then move on to a higher one.

The pressure cooker

When you use a pressure cooker you shorten cooking times appreciably. For example, a beef stew that normally takes 2½ hours gentle simmering needs only 15 minutes at 15 lb. pressure but it naturally takes time to bring the ingredients up to the desired pressure. The manufacturer provides detailed information on using the pressure cooker and cooking times for various dishes, but watch the timing carefully. Even 2–3 minutes overcooking at pressure can spoil vegetables. You will find the pressure cooker invaluable for stocks, soups, stews, and cooking tough cuts of meat.

Appetizers

Do not imagine an appetizer is an extravagance; it can turn a light meal into one that is well balanced nutritionally and more satisfying and interesting. Do not be too conservative about the dishes you choose to start a meal; some families have cheese at the beginning rather than at the end of a meal and I have included an interesting recipe using cheese on page 16.

When you have a fairly filling main dish, appetizers based upon fruit are a wise choice. If your main dish is fish, try having pâté, salami or other cold meat, see pages 22–24. You can adapt many of the recipes in the fish and egg sections of this book to serve at the beginning of a meal, simply by giving smaller portions than you would if they were main courses, and page 18 gives some ideas for making the most of smoked fish.

To Freeze: Have a selection of hors d'oeuvre in your freezer to bring out in the event of unexpected guests. Pack fruit juices into waxed containers with ½ inch "head-room" to allow for expansion of the liquid as it freezes.

Put grapefruit segments in small waxed or plastic containers; I would not sweeten the fruit, then everyone can add as much or as little sugar as they require when eating this.

Dice melon and freeze in syrup. If you buy avocados that are perfect for eating but you cannot use them at once, store in your refrigerator (as far away from the freezing compartment as possible) for one or two days, or freeze, so they do not become overripe. Thaw out at room temperature and use on the same day.

Pâtés can be frozen in well wrapped containers. More information on freezing is given on page 10 and storage time for each dish under each recipe.

Economical appetizers: One of the secrets of economy in menu planning is to use foods in season when they are at their cheapest.

Fresh fruit makes a good hors d'oeuvre, so in addition to the more familiar melon, grapefruit and avocado recipes in this section, try:

Orange and onion salads: Cut thin slices of peeled orange, remove the seeds. Arrange on a bed of shredded lettuce and top with finely chopped green onions or rings of raw onion and well-flavored oil and vinegar dressing.

Fruit suprême: Mix together fresh fruit in season, including fairly sharp citrus fruit. Flavor with a little dry sherry and serve well chilled.

Many countries serve vegetables and salads as separate courses, rather than as an accompaniment to main dishes and this idea can be used to make good meal starters.

Garden salad: Serve plates of wafer-thin slices of cucumber, tomato, red and green peppers (discard seeds), top with an oil and vinegar dressing and a generous amount of chopped parsley, chives, basil and/or tarragon.

Cauliflower salad: Divide a cauliflower into small evenly-sized flowerets. Cook in boiling salted water until just softening; do not over-cook. Drain and blend while still warm with mayonnaise and chopped chives and parsley. Cool and top with more parsley and chopped hard-cooked eggs.

Avocado shrimp cocktail

Avocado Shrimp Cocktail

To make: 10–15 minutes   **No cooking**   **Serves 4**

8 oz. large shrimp
2 avocados
For the French dressing:
½ cup olive oil
3 tablespoons white wine vinegar
1 tablespoon lemon juice
1 teaspoon sugar
¼ teaspoon dry mustard
½ teaspoon salt
freshly ground black pepper
2 teaspoons chopped chives
2 teaspoons chopped parsley
To garnish:
few extra shrimp
Quick tip:
Use 4 oz. cooked, cleaned shrimp and commercially prepared mayonnaise.

Cook shrimp until pink. Shell and devein and place in a bowl. Place all the remaining ingredients, except the extra shrimp and avocados, in a screw-top jar and shake until well mixed. Pour the dressing over the shrimp and marinate 10 minutes. Cut the avocados in halves lengthwise and remove the seeds. Pile the shrimp in the center of each avocado half.
To serve:
Slightly chilled, garnished with the extra shrimp. If preparing some little time before serving, sprinkle the halved avocados with lemon juice.
To vary:
Use any other shellfish and substitute mayonnaise or sauce under Shrimp Cocktail, page 17. Serve filled just with the dressing in the recipe.
To freeze:
Do not freeze this dish; if using frozen shrimp thaw out at room temperature.
To economize:
Use a mixture of flaked cooked white fish and shrimp.

Grapefruit & Melon Cocktail

To make: 10 minutes   **To cook:** 3–4 minutes   **Serves 4–6**

¼ cup sugar
⅔ cup water
1 tablespoon sherry
little ground ginger
2 large grapefruit
½ small melon
Quick tip:
Use canned grapefruit and nearly ⅔ cup syrup from the can; flavor this with sherry and ginger.

Make a syrup by boiling together the sugar and water for 2 minutes. Flavor with the sherry and ginger. Remove sections from the grapefruit; remove the skin and seeds from melon and dice. Mix together and put into glasses. Spoon the syrup over and chill.
To serve:
As the first course of a meal or a dessert.
To vary:
Mix other fruit with the grapefruit and/or melon.
To freeze:
This freezes well. Use within 3–4 months as melon tends to lose some texture.
To economize:
This is an excellent way of using inexpensive melons or one that is slightly damaged.

Melon & Grapes

To make: 10 minutes   **No cooking**   **Serves 4–6**

1 small melon (honeydew or cantaloup)
1 tablespoon sugar
1 lemon
1 small bunch grapes
Quick tip:
Use bottled lemon juice or dry sherry.

Carefully remove the skin and seeds from the melon and cut the melon into cubes, or into balls with a melon baller. Place in a serving bowl, sprinkle with the sugar and squeeze the lemon juice over. Add the seeded grapes.
To serve:
Chilled as an hors d'oeuvre or dessert.
To vary:
Mix other fresh fruit with the melon.
To freeze:
See Grapefruit and Melon Cocktail above.
To economize:
Choose a time when melon is cheapest.

Melon and grapes
Grapefruit and melon cocktail

Stuffed peaches

Avocado Fruit Cocktail

To make: 10 minutes   **No cooking**   **Serves 4–6**

Choose a dressing, see opposite

2 avocados
1 grapefruit
1 orange
1 small lettuce
Quick tip:
Use canned grapefruit and orange
sections.

Place the dressing in a bowl. Halve the avocados, remove the seeds and skin. Dice avocado and place in the dressing immediately so the avocados do not discolor. Cut away the peel and membranes of the grapefruit and orange, dice and add to the avocado mixture. Shred the lettuce finely, put into glasses and top with the avocado mixture.
To serve:
Chilled.
To vary:
Use other fruit in season with avocados or use diced celery and other salad ingredients.
To freeze:
See comments page 12.
To economize:
See To vary:

Stuffed Peaches

To make: 8–10 minutes   **No cooking**   **Serves 4**

2 large ripe peaches or 4 halved
    canned peaches
lemon juice (see method)
3 tablespoons raisins
little boiling water
2 packages (3 oz. each) cream cheese
3 tablespoons chopped walnuts
few lettuce leaves
Quick tip:
Use canned peaches.

If using fresh peaches, halve and sprinkle the cut surface with lemon juice to prevent discoloration. Put the raisins in a bowl. Cover with the water, leave for 4–5 minutes then drain. Mix the cheese, raisins and nuts and make into about 12 small balls. If these balls are very soft, chill the mixture in the refrigerator for a short time. Arrange the peach halves on lettuce leaves and place three cheese balls into each.
To serve:
Well chilled as a light snack or an unusual hors d'oeuvre.
To vary:
Use pears instead of peaches.
To freeze:
Better served freshly made.
To economize:
Use finely grated left-over hard cheese; moisten with a little milk.

Shellfish Cocktails

Most shellfish can be used for these. Crab or lobster should be flaked, but leave shrimp whole. Mix with a dressing (see below), put on finely shredded lettuce and serve as cold as possible.

Green pepper and shrimp cocktail

MARIE ROSE

Mix enough tomato ketchup or tomato paste with mayonnaise to give a delicate tomato flavor. Add seasoning, a few drops of Worcestershire sauce, a squeeze of lemon juice and/or a little sherry, and any other flavoring desired.

CREAM DRESSING

Blend equal quantities of lightly whipped heavy cream and mayonnaise. Add a little extra salt and pepper, a few drops of Tabasco sauce (be careful, this is very hot) and any other flavorings required.

YOGURT DRESSING

This is ideal for slimmers. Season the plain yogurt with salt and pepper, flavor with fresh tomato paste and add a little chopped parsley and lemon juice to flavor.

Green Pepper & Shrimp Cocktails

To make: 10 minutes　**No cooking**　Serves 4–6

4–6 oz. cooked, shelled and deveined shrimp
¼ cup mayonnaise (see page 23)
1 large green pepper
2–3 sticks celery
lettuce
To garnish:
lemon
Quick tip:
Use commercially prepared mayonnaise. Buy frozen shrimp.

Mix the shrimp, mayonnaise, diced green pepper (discard seeds) and the chopped celery. Shred the lettuce finely and put into glasses or on individual dishes. Top with the shrimp mixture and garnish with slices of lemon.
To serve:
As cold as possible, with brown bread and butter.
To vary:
Grapefruit and Shrimp Cocktail: Use sections of fresh or well drained canned grapefruit instead of the pepper and celery. Use diced melon or melon balls in place of the celery. Omit the lettuce. Add a little fresh tomato paste or tomato ketchup to the mayonnaise.
To freeze:
Although the cocktail cannot be frozen, you can use frozen shelled shrimp. Thaw these out at room temperature or see page 10.
To economize:
Mix cooked white fish with a smaller amount of shrimps.

17

Seafood Ramekins

To make: 15 minutes   **To cook:** 15 minutes   **Serves 4**

8 oz. white fish (flounder, cod, sole,
   haddock)
2 cups milk
1 cup mushrooms
3 tablespoons butter
¼ cup flour
4 oz. cooked, shelled and deveined
   shrimps
salt and pepper
juice of ½ a lemon
⅓ cup soft breadcrumbs
3–5 tablespoons grated cheese
To garnish:
½ lemon
1–2 tomatoes
Quick tip:
Omit the mushrooms, butter and
flour and use a can of condensed
cream of mushroom soup instead.
Simmer the fish in ½ cup milk.

Cut the white fish into 1 inch cubes and simmer in the milk for only 5 minutes. Meanwhile wash, but do not peel, the mushrooms and sauté in the hot butter for 2–3 minutes. Stir in the flour, then add the strained liquid from cooking the fish, stir over low heat until thick. Add juice. Spoon into 4 individual dishes or scallop shells, top with the crumbs and cheese and broil until golden. Garnish with lemon and tomato slices and serve at once.

To vary:
Pipe a border of mashed potatoes round the edge of the dish after filling and broil.
   Make pie crust, roll out and line scallop shells, then bake shells; see page 140. Fill with the fish mixture. Bake in a hot oven (400°F.) for 15–20 minutes.

To freeze:
This freezes well for a period of one month.

To economize:
Use all white fish; do not waste stale bread or dry cheese, use for toppings as above.

Smoked Trout Mousse

To make: 15 minutes, plus chilling   **No cooking**   **Serves 4–5**

2 large smoked trout or small
   whitefish
dash black pepper
pinch cayenne pepper
½ teaspoon finely grated lemon rind
½ tablespoon lemon juice
½ cup heavy cream
¼ cup light cream
Quick tip:
Put the fish into a blender and make a
smooth purée.

Remove the skin from the trout and flake the fish, being careful to remove all the bones. Mash the fish until very smooth, then add the peppers, lemon rind and juice and creams, lightly whipped together. Put into small individual dishes and chill thoroughly.

To serve:
With wedges of lemon and brown bread and butter.

To vary:
Use any other smoked fish, see To economize.
   Flavor the mousse with a little horseradish.
   To make an even lighter texture, simmer the fish skin in about 1¼ cups water with salt and pepper to taste for 10 minutes. Strain and save ⅔ cup. Soften, then dissolve 1 teaspoon unflavored gelatin in this liquid, add 1 tablespoon dry sherry. Allow to cool and stiffen slightly, then fold in the flaked fish, then the rest of the ingredients as the recipe above.

To freeze:
The first version, without the gelatin, freezes best. Use within 4–6 weeks.

To economize:
Substitute the cheaper chub or kipper for trout.

Sardine Salad

To make: few minutes   **No cooking**   **Serves 4**

1 large can sardines in oil
1 small lettuce
French dressing (see below)
chopped parsley
grated Parmesan cheese
To garnish:
2 tomatoes
1 lemon
Quick tip:
Use ready-grated cheese.

Open the can of sardines, drain off the oil (this can be used in the French dressing). Arrange the sardines on a bed of shredded lettuce and spoon over the French dressing. Top each sardine with an equal quantity of chopped parsley and Parmesan cheese and garnish the dish with slices of tomato and lemon.

To vary:
Use any other canned or cooked fish in place of sardines.

To freeze:
Left-over sardines could be frozen for 1–2 weeks; do not freeze salad.

Note:
French or Vinaigrette dressing is used in many recipes. Avocado Shrimp Cocktail (page 14) gives the usual proportions of oil and vinegar; vary as wished or add chopped herbs.

Seafood Quiches

To make: 20 minutes   **To cook:** 35 minutes   **Serves 6**

For the flan cases:
3 cups sifted all-purpose flour
pinch salt
1 cup butter
1 egg yolk
water to mix, about ⅓ cup
For the filling:
6 oz. smoked salmon
4 oz. cooked, shelled and deveined
  shrimp
1 tablespoon lemon juice
4 large eggs
⅔ cup light cream
2 cups milk
salt and pepper
chopped parsley
To garnish:
few whole shrimp (optional)
Quick tip:
Use ready frozen pie shells or pie
crust mix.

Seafood quiches

Sift the flour and salt together. Rub in the butter until the mixture resembles fine breadcrumbs. Stir in the egg yolk and water. Knead the pastry lightly on a floured surface, divide into 6 and roll into pieces large enough to line 5-inch deep flan pans or tart pans. Prick the bottom of each pastry shell with a fork and flute the edges. Cut the smoked salmon into 1-inch pieces. Mix the salmon and the shrimp and sprinkle with lemon juice. Beat the eggs, cream and milk together, season with salt and pepper. Divide the salmon and shrimp mixture between the pastry cases, cover with the egg mixture. Bake in a moderately hot oven, 400°F. for 15 minutes. Reduce the temperature to 325°F. and bake another 20 minutes. Sprinkle with chopped parsley before serving. Garnish with a few whole shrimp if desired.

To serve:
Hot or cold as an hors d'oeuvre or light supper dish.
To freeze:
These quiches freeze very well, use within 6 weeks. Reheat from frozen state. If preferred, prepare the pastry, put in the filling and freeze. Cover well then cook from the frozen state.
To economize:
Use flaked cooked white fish or canned pink salmon in place of smoked salmon and shrimp.

Kipper Pâté

2–3 large kippers or 4–6 kipper fillets
water
pepper
1 clove garlic
¼ cup butter
juice of 1 lemon
little light cream
To garnish:
few lettuce leaves
lemon
Quick tip:
Use uncooked kipper (see To vary).

Put the kippers into a large container. Pour over boiling water to cover and leave for 5 minutes only. Remove from the liquid and take out any bones, then flake finely, or put into the blender to make a smooth mixture. Do not try to put too much fish into the blender at one time. Add the pepper, finely crushed garlic and melted butter and beat well, then add the lemon juice and enough cream to make a soft consistency. Put into small individual containers or one larger dish. Chill thoroughly.
To serve:
Unmold and garnish with lettuce and wedges of lemon.
To vary:
Omit the cream and blend uncooked, flaked kipper with ½ cup cream cheese or cottage cheese and finely diced gherkins. This makes a delicious pâté.
To freeze:
Wrap well and freeze. Use within 4–6 weeks.
To economize:
Use homogenized milk instead of cream.

Spanish Salad

1 tablespoon olive oil
½ cup long-grain rice
1¼ cups cold water
salt and pepper
1 green pepper
1 red pepper
⅓ cup mayonnaise
few sliced stuffed olives
3 tomatoes
1½ cups mixed cooked, diced
    chicken, ham or other cooked meat
    (see method), canned anchovies
    and shrimp
few lettuce leaves
Quick tip:
Cook extra rice when serving boiled rice hot, save and reheat for a salad.

Heat the oil and toss the rice in the hot oil, then add the water and salt and pepper. Bring the liquid to a boil, stir briskly, cover the pan, lower the heat and simmer for 15 minutes, by which time most of the liquid should have evaporated. Remove from the heat. Dice the peppers (discarding seeds) and add to the rice with the mayonnaise while the rice is still hot. Allow to cool, then stir in the sliced olives, skinned sliced tomatoes and any cooked chicken, ham or other meat, anchovies and shrimp. This is a salad in which you can have a mixture of fish and meat. Serve on a bed of lettuce.
To vary:
Omit the peppers and add cooked diced carrots and cooked peas.
To freeze:
The rice mixture can be frozen, see page 102.
To economize:
Use small portions of left-over fish, etc.

Mediterranean Stuffed Tomatoes

4 large or 6 medium-sized firm
    tomatoes
salt and pepper
2 cups soft breadcrumbs
1 medium-sized onion
1 clove garlic
¾ cup mushrooms
8 blanched almonds
1 tablespoon chopped parsley
2 tablespoons butter
To garnish:
black olives
Quick tip:
Use about 2 oz. herb stuffing mix and mix with the mushrooms, nuts and parsley.

Cut the tomatoes in half and scoop out the insides. Season the insides with salt and pepper and turn the tomatoes upside down on a board or plate to drain while preparing the stuffing. Chop the tomato pulp finely and mix with the breadcrumbs, grated onion, crushed garlic, finely chopped mushrooms, chopped almonds and parsley. Season with salt and pepper. Pile the mixture into the tomato cases. Put a small piece of butter on top of each stuffed tomato and place in an ovenproof dish. Bake, uncovered, in a moderate oven, 350°F. until golden brown, about 15–20 minutes. Garnish each tomato with a whole or halved olive.
To serve:
As an appetizer or light supper dish.
To vary:
Omit the mushrooms and add grated Cheddar cheese.
To freeze:
Do not freeze this dish.
To economize:
Use 2½ tablespoons chopped peanuts in place of the almonds.

Mediterranean stuffed tomatoes

Meat Appetizers

There are many ways in which meat can be served at the beginning of a meal. It is often a good way to use up small portions of meat that would be insufficient for a main dish.

Chopped liver: Buy chicken livers or other tender liver, i.e., calf or lamb. Slice thinly and fry in hot chicken fat or butter with a finely chopped onion for a few minutes. Season, then chop very finely and blend with chopped hard-cooked egg yolks. Place on lettuce and top with the chopped hard-cooked egg whites.

Ham mousse: Follow the directions for the Smoked Trout Mousse on page 18, but flavor with mustard as well as lemon juice. If using the recipe with gelatin, dissolve this in ⅔ cup tomato juice or unsalted stock.

Ham rolls: Spread thin slices of cooked ham with cream cheese or mayonnaise, flavored with mustard or horseradish. Lay an asparagus tip on the ham and roll up firmly. Serve on a bed of lettuce. This can be varied, as you will see from the recipe opposite. Another good filling for the rolls would be a home-made or canned pâté.

Beef spread: Simmer ground round in enough seasoned water to cover. When nearly tender, remove the pan lid, so the excess liquid evaporates. Blend each 1 lb. beef with ¼ cup butter, grated nutmeg and sherry or brandy to flavor. Anchovy fillets are a traditional addition to beef spread; simmer the beef with pepper, but little, if any salt, add the butter and chopped anchovy fillets.

Salami cornucopias: Blend cream cheese with finely chopped walnuts. Spread on slices of salami, then roll into cornucopia. Secure with toothpicks until just ready to serve.

Sour sweet tongue: Dice cooked tongue (the canned lambs' tongues are ideal). Blend with equal quantities of a sweet chutney and finely chopped cocktail onions or pickles. Serve on a bed of lettuce and garnish with "fans" of gherkin.

Sour sweet sausages: Use sliced cooked sausages or frankfurters instead of the tongue above.

Ham, tuna and fennel appetizer

Ham, Tuna & Fennel Appetizer

To make: 10 minutes   **No cooking**   **Serves 4**

4 large slices lean ham
1 can (7 oz.) tuna
⅔ cup mayonnaise
¼ cup grated or finely chopped fresh
  fennel
12 black olives
1 canned pimiento
To garnish:
parsley
Quick tip:
Grate the fennel, instead of chopping.
To economize:
Use boiled ham, canned ham or
luncheon meat and cut into
neat fingers.

Tuna combines with most other ingredients and here is teamed with anise-flavored fennel and mild, lean ham for an interesting salad. Halve the slices of ham, roll neatly and put on a flat serving dish. Drain the tuna and break into small chunks. Spoon tuna on top of the ham. Combine the mayonnaise and fennel together. Spoon over the tuna then stud with olives. Cut the pimiento into thin strips and decorate the rolls with a criss-cross of pimiento. Garnish with parsley.
To serve:
As a light main dish or appetizer to a meal.
To vary:
Spread the slices of ham with cottage or cream cheese, blended with chopped olives, then roll.
To freeze:
Do not freeze this dish.

Deviled Crab

To make: 15–20 minutes   **To cook:** 3–4 minutes   **Serves 4**

1 can (6½ oz.) crabmeat or 1 large
  crab, cooked
¼ cup butter
1 teaspoon prepared mustard
pinch curry powder
½ teaspoon Worcestershire sauce
1 cup soft breadcrumbs
¼ cup mayonnaise
salt and pepper
Quick tip:
Use the canned crabmeat.
To economize:
Use a mixture of flaked white fish
and a small quantity of crab.

Open the can of crabmeat, drain and flake, removing shells. Mix the crab with half the softened butter, the mustard, curry powder, Worcestershire sauce, half the breadcrumbs and the mayonnaise. Season with salt and pepper. Put into one shallow dish or four individual scallop shells and top with the remaining crumbs and butter. Brown slowly under a broiler and serve hot.
To vary:
Omit mustard and curry powder and add tomato paste to taste.
To freeze:
Prepare, but do not cook; freeze then cover. Use within 1 month.

Home-made mayonnaise

If making this by hand or with an electric whisk put 1 egg yolk into a dry bowl with salt and pepper to taste, a good pinch of sugar and ½–1 teaspoon prepared mustard. Add up to ⅔ cup oil drop by drop, whisking steadily or beating with a wooden spoon. Beat in 1–2 tablespoons vinegar or lemon juice plus ½ tablespoon hot water. If making in a blender put in the egg yolk, seasonings and vinegar or lemon juice. Switch on for few seconds, then add the oil steadily through the hole in the cap or foil funnel, see page 11, at medium speed, adding the water at the end.

Bacon & Shrimp Kebabs

To make: 10 minutes   **To cook:** 5–6 minutes   **Serves 4**

8 slices bacon
32 cooked, shelled and deveined
  shrimp
To garnish:
few lettuce leaves
lemon
Quick tip:
It is not quicker to cook in the oven but much easier for a party. Place skewers on a rack so the excess fat runs away. Cook quickly without turning.
To economize:
Use cooked mussels instead
of shrimps.

Stretch the bacon slices by stroking them firmly with the back of a knife, then divide each slice into 4 pieces. Roll each piece around shrimp. Put on 4 metal skewers and cook under a broiler until the bacon is crisp, turning once or twice during cooking. Serve hot, garnished with lettuce and wedges of lemon.
To vary:
Devils on Horseback: Roll halved bacon slices round pitted prunes and cook as above. Serve on toast as a hot hors d'oeuvre.
Angels on Horseback: Roll halved bacon slices round well seasoned oysters. Serve on toast as a hot hors d'oeuvre.
Note:
Secure the bacon round the prunes or oysters with toothpicks or put on skewers as the recipe for kebabs.
To freeze:
Use frozen shrimp and thaw out before cooking. Do not freeze the cooked dish.

Pâtés

Pâtés are an interesting hors d'oeuvre which can be prepared well ahead.
Quick tip:
Put the ingredients into a blender to mix. Remember though to blend small amounts at a time and to put in any liquid (such as melted butter) before the solid liver.

To serve:
With hot toast and butter.
To freeze:
Cover the top of the cool pâté with melted butter, wrap and freeze. Use within 6 weeks. The tongue pâté only freezes when the eggs are sieved; even chopped hard-cooked eggs become like rubber when frozen.
To economize:
Simmer cheaper beef heart in a little stock. When tender grind finely and use in the pâté. Follow the recipe, but use double the amount of butter to give a richer flavor.

Liver Pâté

To make: 10 minutes   **To cook:** 6–10 minutes   **Serves 5–6**

12 oz. calf, lamb, pig or mixed livers
½ cup butter
1 clove garlic
1 small onion
3–4 tablespoons stock
3–4 tablespoons light cream
1 tablespoon sherry
salt and pepper
To garnish:
parsley

If you are not using a blender, mince the raw liver or chop very finely. If you are using a blender, see Quick tip, given above. Melt half the butter in a large pan and sauté the minced liver in this for about 5 minutes, together with the crushed clove of garlic and grated onion; add the stock during cooking so the liver keeps very moist. Pour into a large bowl. Then add the rest of the butter, cream, sherry, salt and pepper. Mix very thoroughly, cover and chill to set. If you have a blender you can cut the liver into thin slices, cook, then blend as directions above. Turn into 1 large or several smaller dishes and garnish with parsley.

Tongue Pâté

To make: 10 minutes   **To cook:** 10 minutes   **Serves 5–6**

2 eggs
8 oz. diced, cooked tongue
¼ cup butter
¼ cup light cream
1 tablespoon finely chopped chives
1 tablespoon brandy
salt and pepper

Put the eggs on to hard-cook, then plunge into cold water at the end of 10 minutes to prevent a dark line forming around the yolks. Try to use them while warm as they are easier to blend. Cut the tongue into small pieces and soften the butter. Put the tongue, butter and chopped eggs into a bowl and beat in cream, chives and brandy. Season to taste with salt and pepper. If preferred, use a blender, see Quick tip, above. Chill.

Speedy Liver Pâté

To make: 10 minutes   **No cooking   Serves 4–6**

8 oz. liverwurst or liver sausage
2 tablespoons butter
¼ cup cream cheese
2–3 gherkins
2–3 cocktail onions
½–1 teaspoon prepared mustard

Soften the liverwurst and blend with the butter and cream cheese. Add the finely chopped gherkins and onions, together with the mustard. Press into a buttered dish, cover with foil and chill. If preferred, use a blender, see Quick tip above.
To vary:
Use freshly cooked minced liver instead of the liverwurst. Add chopped parsley or other chopped herbs.

Russian Salad

To make: 25 minutes   **To cook:** 20–25 minutes   **Serves 4–6**

1 lb. mixed root vegetables (carrots, turnips, potatoes)
salt and pepper
⅔ cup mayonnaise (see page 23)
1–2 tablespoons chopped parsley
Quick tip:
Use cooked frozen or well drained canned vegetables.
To economize:
Use the cheaper parsnips, yellow turnips.

Prepare and dice the vegetables. Cook in boiling salted water until just tender; do not over-cook as the vegetables soften slightly as they cool. Drain well, blend with the mayonnaise and half the parsley. Allow to cool and top with more parsley. Chill.
To serve:
As part of an hors d'oeuvre.
To vary:
The original Russian salad had diced cooked tongue added and this makes a hearty first course. You can also add diced cooked ham and chopped hard-cooked eggs.
To freeze:
While you can freeze the cooked vegetables, see page 100, it is not satisfactory to freeze the salad.

Herring Salad

4 rollmop herrings
2 apples
2–3 gherkins or piece cucumber
2 teaspoons capers
3 tablespoons French dressing (see page 14)
3 tablespoons mayonnaise (see page 23)
few lettuce leaves
To garnish:
watercress
diced beets
Quick tip:
Grate rather than dice the apples and cucumber.

Drain the herrings and cut into narrow strips, peel and dice the apples, dice the gherkins or cucumber. Mix the herrings, apples, gherkins or cucumber, capers, dressing and mayonnaise. Chill. Spoon on lettuce just before serving and garnish with watercress and diced beets.
To serve:
By itself or as part of an hors d'oeuvre.
To vary:
Use other pickled herrings with rather more French dressing.
To freeze:
The salad cannot be frozen.

Russian salad

Egg Dishes

Eggs form an essential part of most mixed hors d'oeuvre. They can be hard-cooked, sliced and topped with mayonnaise, or served whole with a coating of mayonnaise and garnished with strips of pimiento, anchovy fillets or smoked salmon, as in Nova Scotia Eggs.

Scrambled eggs can be blended with mayonnaise or cream as in Stuffed Mushrooms.

Bake eggs in individual dishes with salt and pepper, cream, diced smoked or cooked salmon, asparagus tips or grated cheese, or cook in tomato cases as in Cheese and Tomato Meringues, opposite.

Crunchy Tomato & Egg Pie

For the pie crust:
1½ cups crushed cornflakes
salt and pepper
6 tablespoons butter
6 tablespoons grated Cheddar cheese
For the filling:
3–4 eggs
1 envelope unflavored gelatin
2 tablespoons cold water
1¼ cups tomato juice
3–4 green onions or 1 small onion
½ small cucumber
¾ cup grated Cheddar cheese
Quick tip:
Stand the tomato mixture on a bed of crushed ice to set quickly, or place the mixture into the freezer for about 20–30 minutes; do not forget it, as the eggs and cucumber are spoiled by freezing.

To make: 15 minutes   **To cook:** 10 minutes   **Serves 6**

Mix the crushed cornflakes, salt and pepper, slightly softened butter and cheese. Press into bottom and sides of an ungreased 8 inch pan. Bake for approximately 10 minutes in moderate oven (350°F.). Allow to cool. Meanwhile hard-cook the eggs. Soften the gelatin in cold water, then stand over a pan of hot water, stirring until dissolved. Stir in the tomato juice, chill until thickened slightly, then stir in the finely chopped onion, diced cucumber, cheese and two of the eggs, finely chopped. Pour into the pie shell. Chill until firm. Chop the remaining egg white and yolk separately, and arrange around the edge of the pie.
To freeze:
This dish cannot be frozen as the chopped hard-cooked eggs would become tough, and the cucumber and onion would lose their crisp texture.
To economize:
This is a very good way of using small pieces of cheese, a few onions, etc. that are left over. If you have some left-over tomatoes, cook these with a little water, then rub through a sieve and use in place of the tomato juice. Another way to give a tomato flavor is to blend 1 tablespoon tomato paste with chicken stock or water and ½ a chicken bouillon cube. This gives a pleasantly piquant taste.

Nova Scotia Eggs

4 eggs
4 thin slices smoked salmon
juice of 1 large lemon
approximately ½ cup mayonnaise
3 tablespoons heavy cream
To garnish:
shredded lettuce
sliced lemon
Quick tip:
Poach eggs for 2 minutes instead of boiling.

To make: 5 minutes   **To cook:** 4–5 minutes   **Serves 4**

Place the eggs gently in a pan of boiling water and boil gently for 4–5 minutes. Plunge into a bowl of cold water immediately. When cold, remove shells carefully. Lay slices of smoked salmon on individual plates, sprinkle with half the lemon juice. Place an egg on the center of each slice of smoked salmon. Blend the mayonnaise and cream, flavor with remaining lemon juice. Coat each egg completely with 3 tablespoons mayonnaise mixture. Refrigerate until ready to serve.
To serve:
With shredded lettuce around each egg and a slice of lemon.
To vary:
Eggs Benedict: A simplified version of this classic dish can be made by putting the shelled eggs on a slice of ham and coating them with mayonnaise. The classic dish is made by coating hot poached eggs or lightly cooked shelled eggs with Hollandaise sauce.

To make enough Hollandaise sauce to coat the eggs: Put 2 egg yolks, ½–1 tablespoon lemon juice or white wine vinegar and salt and pepper into a bowl. Stand over a pan of hot water, whisk sharply until thick and creamy. Gradually beat ¼ cup softened butter into the sauce.

Paprika eggs: Blend ½–1 teaspoon paprika into mayonnaise or Hollandaise sauce, made as above, then spoon over the cooked eggs. Serve on slices of smoked salmon or ham and garnish with strips of pimiento.
To freeze:
Do not freeze this dish, although frozen smoked salmon can be used, see page 52. Hard-cooked eggs are one of the foods that cannot be frozen; they become very "rubbery".
To economize:
Use portions of smoked kipper or trout instead of salmon.

Stuffed Mushrooms

To make: 10 minutes   **To cook:** 10 minutes   **Serves 4–6**

about 16–18 good-sized mushrooms
6 tablespoons butter
salt and pepper
3 eggs
3 tablespoons mayonnaise or heavy
   cream
little grated cheese (optional)
2 teaspoons chopped chives
Quick tip:
Use well drained canned mushrooms
and spoon the egg mixture over the
top of them.

Wash the mushrooms, but do not peel them. Remove the stems and chop finely. Heat half the butter in a pan, fry the mushroom caps until tender, season with salt and pepper and keep hot. Melt the remaining butter and fry the stems for 2–3 minutes. Pour in the beaten and seasoned eggs and scramble lightly. Add the rest of the ingredients when the eggs are nearly set. Spoon the mixture into the mushroom caps. Serve at once.
To vary:
Serve cold. Sprinkle well drained mushrooms with French dressing, page 14. Arrange on a bed of lettuce, then fill with egg mixture; make this a little more moist as it stiffens as it cools.
To freeze:
Do not freeze the cooked dish, but you can use frozen mushroom, thawed.

Cheese & Tomato Meringues

To make: 10 minutes   **To cook:** 15 minutes   **Serves 4**

4 large tomatoes
2 tablespoons butter
4 eggs, separated
salt and pepper
⅓ cup grated Parmesan cheese
1 tablespoon chopped chives or
   parsley
Quick tip:
Buy ready grated Parmesan.

Make sure the tomatoes stand quite firmly, then cut a slice from the top of each tomato. Scoop out the pulp with a teaspoon, chop this finely and mix with the softened butter, egg yolks, salt and pepper. Add half the cheese and half the herbs. Pour the mixture back into the tomato cases. If you have a little too much mixture, put the extra into a small dish. Put the tomatoes into an ovenproof dish, cook for 10 minutes in a moderately hot oven, 400°F. Beat the egg whites until stiff, fold in the salt and pepper and remaining cheese and herbs. Remove tomatoes from oven, top with the meringue, lower the heat to moderate, 350°F. and bake for a further 5 minutes. Serve at once.

Cheese and tomato meringues

Soups

While there are excellent ready made soups on the market, it is both easy and economical to make some soups at home. This chapter gives interesting and varied recipes.

Take advantage of vegetables in season to produce nutritious soups, which can be made in minutes and try new ideas with fish or meat. Remember too that chilled soups can be delicious.

A blender saves valuable time as when a recipe states "sieve" the ingredients, you can make a smooth purée. It does not, however, remove all traces of skin and seeds from tomatoes, etc.

Some soups depend upon stock for flavor; it is easy to make this, simply cover bones with water, add salt and pepper, herbs and vegetables to flavor (although these are not essential). Simmer gently for several hours. To save energy, make the stock in a covered container in the oven when you are cooking other dishes at a low temperature.

Stock is highly perishable so store in the refrigerator and use as soon as possible, particularly if it contains vegetables. Boil thoroughly when using this.

To freeze: Most soups freeze well but use within

the time recommended in the recipe. Freeze stock, as the picture below. Make the stock, strain, cool and pour into freezing trays, as though making ice cubes. When frozen remove the cubes and store in a suitable container. Add as many as required to flavor the soup. Use frozen stock within 3 months.

Vegetable soups: There are so many good soups to be made with vegetables and every month of the year produces a different variety to use. Treat the vegetable soup recipes (pages 30–36) as basic ideas and change the vegetables according to the season.

Remember to taste as you make the soup, and season wisely; add enough well flavored vegetables (onions, leeks, etc.) for a good definite taste in vegetable soups. Use a bouquet garni in many soups; this is a selection of herbs (parsley, chives, tarragon, dill) tied either into a small bunch or in a muslin bag. Remove these before you serve the soup, although they can be strained or put into the blender (without the muslin bag or string) with the rest of the vegetables if you feel the soup needs the extra interest. Garlic not only adds its own taste but helps to "bring out" the flavor of onions and other ingredients.

The picture opposite shows one of the best known vegetable soups, the classic French Onion Soup. You will find the recipe on page 30.

If you are in a hurry, grate the prepared vegetables so they cook quickly and retain the maximum flavor and nutrients.

Economical soups: Never waste left-over meat, fish or vegetables, for they can form the basis of interesting soups; the recipes in this section will give you ideas for using these.

French onion soup

10 Minute Vegetable Soup

1 lb. mixed vegetables
3 cups chicken stock or water and 2 chicken bouillon cubes
bouquet garni (see page 28)
salt and pepper
1 tablespoon chopped parsley
Quick tip:
Use the blender (see method) or use frozen mixed vegetables.

Peel the vegetables. Either grate, put through a shredder or drop into the blender (use a small quantity of the liquid, and follow the manufacturer's instructions for tiny pieces of vegetable). Meanwhile bring the stock or water to the boil. Add the vegetables, bouillon cubes, if using these, bouquet garni and salt and pepper. Cook quickly for 6–7 minutes or until the vegetables are tender. Remove the bouquet garni. Top with parsley and serve very hot.

To vary:
Cook as above and purée the soup, either sieve or put into a blender. There is no need to cut the vegetables into such small pieces if puréeing.

To freeze:
The soup freezes well. Use within 3 months.

To economize:
Choose vegetables in season.

Creamed Vegetable Soup

1 lb. vegetables*
¼ cup butter or margarine
2½ cups chicken stock or water and 2 chicken bouillon cubes
bouquet garni (see page 28)
salt and pepper
¼ cup flour
1¼ cups milk
¼ cup light cream
1 tablespoon chopped parsley
*If using very starchy vegetables such as potatoes, and making a purée, reduce this quantity to just over 8 oz. otherwise the soup will be too thick.
Quick tip:
Use the blender to make the purée.

Prepare and dice the vegetables; if you do not want to make a purée, follow the directions for grating in the recipe above. Sauté the vegetables in half the butter or margarine then add the stock or water and bouillon cube, and bouquet garni. Season lightly with salt and pepper and simmer for about 15 minutes. When the vegetables are tender, sieve or put into the blender. Remove the bouquet garni or sieve or blend with the vegetables. Meanwhile make a white sauce with the rest of the butter or margarine, flour and milk, see page 55. Mix the vegetables and liquid, or the vegetable purée, with the hot sauce and reheat; add extra salt and pepper if desired and the cream. Top with parsley and serve hot.

To freeze:
This soup can separate during freezing. It is better to freeze the vegetable mixture and complete the soup before serving.

To economize:
Use inexpensive vegetables — carrots, potatoes, turnips.

French Onion Soup

3 large onions
2 cloves garlic (optional)
2 tablespoons butter
1 tablespoon olive oil
5 cups beef stock or water and 4 beef bouillon cubes
salt and pepper
4–6 rounds French bread
½ cup grated Gruyère or Cheddar cheese
Quick tip:
Cook instant minced onions in canned beef consommé or in water and bouillon cubes. Top with bread and cheese as the recipe.

Peel the onions and cut into thin slices, then chop these slices so the portions of onion are easy to eat. Peel and crush the garlic, if using this. Heat the butter and oil and sauté the onions and garlic in this until a pale golden brown. Add the stock or water and bouillon cubes and salt and pepper; for this soup it is important to have a well flavored stock. Cover the pan and simmer for 25–30 minutes. Meanwhile toast the bread, then top with the cheese. Spoon the soup into a flameproof dish, top with the bread and broil for 1–2 minutes or until cheese melts and browns. Serve hot.

To vary:
When the onions are cooked the soup could be sieved or whirled in a blender.

To freeze:
This soup is excellent when frozen although some people find the garlic loses its potency, see page 10, so add crushed garlic when reheating if you require a stronger flavor.

To economize:
Never waste good beef bones (or other bones); simmer to give stock.

Bortsch

1 clove garlic
1 onion
1 tablespoon oil or margarine
6 oz. stewing beef (chuck)
5 cups cold water
salt and pepper
1 bay leaf
½–1 tablespoon chopped fresh thyme
    or ½–1 teaspoon dried thyme
1 carrot
½ small yellow turnip
¼ green cabbage
2 raw medium-sized beets
2 tomatoes
few drops vinegar or lemon juice
little sour cream or yogurt

Quick tip:
Use cooked beets, peel, grate and add to soup with the tomatoes (see variations).

To vary:
Omit the meat and use beef stock or water and 1–2 beef bouillon cubes. This means the cooking time can be reduced by 1 hour.

Ten-minute bortsch:
Put 3¾ cups beef stock or water and 2 beef bouillon cubes into a pan. Add 2 large grated cooked beets, 1 grated onion, 1 grated carrot, 1 crushed clove garlic, salt and pepper, a little lemon juice or vinegar, pinch dried thyme and celery salt. Simmer quickly for 10 minutes. Serve hot or cold.

Cranberry bortsch:
Russian cooks make a delicious soup with cranberries instead of beets. Follow recipe for Ten-minute Bortsch, using 1 cup fresh cranberries instead of beets.

To freeze:
This freezes well, use within 3 months; add sour cream or yogurt when serving the soup. Use within 2 months if making and freezing the quick Bortsch.

To economize:
Make larger quantities of this soup when beets are at their cheapest and freeze.

  You save time and money on energy if you cook this soup in a pressure cooker. Use just over half the amount of water in the recipe and allow 25 minutes at 15 lb. pressure. Allow pressure to drop at room temperature.

Peel and chop the garlic and onion. Fry slowly in the oil or margarine until golden. Remove fat and coarse tissues from beef and cut into ½ inch cubes. Add the meat to the pan and fry lightly until brown. Add the cold water, salt and pepper, bay leaf and thyme, cover and bring to a boil. Reduce heat and simmer gently for 30 minutes. Meanwhile, slice the carrot, turnip and cabbage, peel and grate the raw beets and add to pan. Return to a boil and simmer for 1 hour. Skin and chop the tomatoes, add to the pan and simmer for a further 20 minutes. Flavor the soup with vinegar or lemon juice to taste.

To serve:
Hot or cold, topped with sour cream or yogurt.

Bortsch

Minestrone

8 oz. navy beans
8 oz. salt pork
1 onion
2 cloves garlic
5 pints beef stock or water and 8 beef
    bouillon cubes
2 carrots
2 sticks celery
salt and pepper
1 cup peas, fresh or frozen
1 cup green beans
2 tomatoes
¼ green cabbage
1 cup ditali macaroni
2 tablespoons chopped parsley

To garnish:
1 cup (4 oz.) grated Parmesan cheese

Quick tip:
Omit the dried navy beans and add
canned cannelloni beans or baked
beans in tomato sauce to the soup
towards the end of the cooking
period.

To freeze:
This soup freezes well for a limited
period, after this the pasta tends to
lose its texture. Use within 2 months.
If, however, you make the soup
without the macaroni you can store it
for 4 months. Add a little cooked
macaroni when reheating the soup, or
add a little extra water or stock to the
soup when heating, put in the
uncooked macaroni and continue
cooking until this is tender.

To economize:
Serve generous portions of this soup
as a light main meal with a generous
amount of cheese to provide the
protein. Use left-over pieces of cheese
instead of buying Parmesan cheese.

Speedy minestrone:
Heat 1¼ cups water in a good sized
pan, add 1 beef bouillon cube. Stir in 1
package (10 oz.) frozen mixed
vegetables, cook until nearly tender.
Add the contents of a small to
medium-sized can of both baked
beans and spaghetti in tomato sauce
(chop the spaghetti into smaller
pieces). Heat well, then top with
chopped parsley.
　　Do not try to freeze this version of
Minestrone soup for the ingredients
would become over-soft with storage.
It is also pointless since the soup is
prepared so quickly.

Soak navy beans in cold water overnight for 12 hours. Drain, place in a
clean pan with cold water to cover, put a lid on the pan and simmer for 1½
hours. Drain well.
　　Remove skin from the pork and cut pork into ½ inch cubes. Place diced
pork in a large heavy pan, cover and fry in its own fat until brown, shaking
the pan occasionally. Add the chopped onion and garlic and fry until soft.
Add the stock or water and beef bouillon cubes, drained navy beans, sliced
carrots and celery and salt and pepper; do not add too much salt. Cover and
bring to a boil, reduce heat and simmer soup for 1½ hours. Add peas,
green beans broken into large pieces, skinned and chopped tomatoes,
shredded cabbage and macaroni. Simmer for a further 15–20 minutes or
until the macaroni is tender. More water may be added at this stage if the
soup is too thick. Taste the soup and add more salt and pepper if necessary.
Stir in the chopped parsley just before serving.

To serve:
Hot, sprinkled with Parmesan cheese.
　　This is the type of soup that can be served as a light main dish, for it is
very satisfying and the peas, beans and cheese provide an adequate
amount of protein.

To vary:
Use half stock and half tomato juice for a more pronounced tomato flavor
and a very pleasant color to the soup. The fresh tomatoes could then be
omitted.

Minestrone soup

Tomato Chowder

To make: 15 minutes   **To cook:** 25 minutes   **Serves 4–6**

2–3 slices bacon
2–3 medium-sized onions
3 cups water
2–3 medium-sized potatoes
4 large tomatoes
pinch dried basil or ½–1 tablespoon
   chopped fresh basil
salt and pepper
little heavy cream
To garnish:
chopped chives
Quick tip:
Use 1–2 tablespoons instant minced
onions, canned potatoes and canned
tomatoes (use liquid from can and less
water).

Chop the bacon into small pieces. Fry the bacon and chopped onions for a few minutes. Add the water, bring to a boil, then put in the diced potatoes, skinned and chopped tomatoes, herbs and salt and pepper. Simmer until the vegetables are tender (approximately 12 minutes). Spoon into hot soup cups (this is a very thick soup, almost like a stew) and top with cream and chives.
To serve:
Hot with crisp rolls or toast.
To vary:
Use less potatoes and add cooked or canned kernel corn.
   Fry 1–2 cloves crushed garlic with the bacon and onions.
To freeze:
Although this soup can be frozen, I prefer the texture when it is freshly cooked and served.
To economize:
Use any "odd" pieces of bacon and buy less perfect shaped tomatoes (which are always slightly cheaper).

Tomato & Onion Soup

To make: 25 minutes   **To cook:** 25 minutes   **Serves 4–6**

2 large onions
1–2 cloves garlic (optional)
3 tablespoons oil or ¼ cup butter or
   margarine
1 red pepper
3¾ cups brown or white stock or
   water
3 large tomatoes
4 oz. mushrooms
salt and pepper
To garnish:
chopped herbs, grated cheese or
   croûtons
Quick tip:
Use canned tomatoes, 3 tablespoons
instant minced onion and 1 canned
pimiento.

Peel the onions and cut into thin slices. Peel and crush the garlic cloves, if using. Heat the oil, butter or margarine and sauté the onion and garlic in this until nearly transparent; take care the onions do not brown. Discard the seeds from the pepper, and cut the flesh into thin strips. Mix with the onion but do not fry if you like a firm texture. Add the stock or water, bring to a boil. Skin and chop the tomatoes, slice the mushrooms and add to the pan. Continue simmering until the vegetables are soft, season with salt and pepper.
To serve:
While very hot. Garnish with chopped fresh herbs, grated cheese or croûtons.
To vary:
Use all onions.
   Use all mushrooms.
To freeze:
Excellent, use within 3 months.
To economize:
Omit red pepper. Turn this into a light, complete meal by adding any tiny pieces of left-over cooked chicken.

Cucumber Soup

To make: 10 minutes   **To cook:** 20 minutes   **Serves 4–6**

2 small or 1 large cucumber
1 onion
¼ cup butter
3¾ cups stock or water and 3 chicken
   bouillon cubes
salt and pepper
⅔ cup heavy cream
Quick tip:
Put the stock and large pieces of
vegetables into the blender, switch on
for a few seconds only, then continue
as the recipe.

Peel and chop nearly all the cucumber. Put a small piece on one side to slice for garnish and retain a small portion of the peel to give color and additional flavor to the soup; too much peel gives a bitter taste. Peel and chop the onion. Sauté the vegetables in the hot butter for a few minutes; take care they do not brown. Add the stock or water and bouillon cubes, the pieces of cucumber peel and a little salt and pepper. Simmer for 20 minutes, then whirl in a blender or sieve. Heat, then stir in the cream.
To serve:
Hot, or chill well.
To vary:
Add a pinch of curry powder to the soup.
   Use a little white wine in place of some of the stock.
To freeze:
While this soup can be frozen for 2–3 weeks, it is not the most satisfactory soup for this purpose.
To economize:
Use white sauce instead of cream.

Cold Soups

Many soups are equally good hot or cold, some rather surprisingly such as Mulligatawny which is delicious served well chilled. Most cold soups can be topped with sour cream or yogurt just before serving.

Cucumber Yogurt Soup

To make: 10 minutes   **No cooking**   **Serves 4–6**

1 small cucumber
1¼ cups plain yogurt
milk or stock (see method)
salt and pepper

Peel and grate the cucumber, blend with the yogurt and enough milk or stock to give the consistency of light cream, season with salt and pepper.
To vary:
Flavor the soup with chopped green onions or chives, curry powder or a little chopped mint.

Chilled Avocado Soup

To make: 10 minutes   **No cooking**   **Serves 4–6**

2 large or 3 medium-sized ripe
    avocados
juice of 1 lemon
2½ cups home-made beef or chicken
    stock or water and 2 chicken
    bouillon cubes
⅔ cup plain yogurt
salt and pepper
To garnish:
chopped chives or green onions
Quick tip:
Use the blender as suggested in the recipe.

Halve the avocados, remove seeds, scoop out the pulp and rub through a nylon sieve, using a wooden spoon. Blend in the remaining ingredients at once, except the chives or green onions and season well.
    If preferred, place all the ingredients (but not the chives or onions) in a blender and whirl at high speed until the mixture is smooth.
To serve:
Chilled, topped with a few chopped chives or chopped green onions.
To vary:
Flavor with a little curry powder or Tabasco sauce.
To freeze:
This freezes excellently; use within 2–3 months. If the mixture shows signs of separating when it defrosts, beat until smooth.
To economize:
Often one can buy avocados that are slightly damaged or overripe at a cheaper price; discard damaged part and use remainder.

Orange & Apple Soup

To make: 15 minutes   **To cook:** 15 minutes   **Serves 4**

1 medium-sized onion
⅔ cup chicken stock
1¼ cups hard cider
1¼ cups orange juice
little sugar (see method)
salt and pepper
1 stick cinnamon or pinch ground
    cinnamon
To garnish:
2 apples
Quick tip:
Use 2 teaspoons instant minced onion and canned orange juice.
To economize:
Use stock with a little lemon juice instead of cider.

Chop the onion and heat for 5 minutes in the stock. Cover the pan and leave until the stock is cold then strain the liquid into the cider and orange juice. Add a little sugar and enough salt and pepper to make an interesting taste. Add the cinnamon and chill until ready to serve. Remove the cinnamon stick.
To serve:
In cold soup cups, topped with finely diced peeled apple. Serve rye bread with the soup.
To freeze:
Although you can freeze the soup it is better freshly made; you can, however, use frozen orange juice, see page 12.

Chilled avocado soup

Chilled Asparagus Almond Soup

To make: 10–15 minutes   **To cook:** 25 minutes   **Serves 6**

1 lb. fresh asparagus
salt and pepper
6¼ cups chicken stock or water and 5
    chicken bouillon cubes
½ cup ground blanched almonds
Quick tip:
Use canned asparagus and freshly
blanched and ground almonds for a
good flavor. However, if you use
commercially prepared almonds, this
soup is very quick to make.

Cook the asparagus in salted water until tender. Reserve some of the asparagus tips for garnish. Put the remaining asparagus and half the chicken stock or water and bouillon cubes in a blender and mix to a purée, or sieve the asparagus and mix with the stock. Place purée, remaining stock, ground almonds and salt and pepper in a large pan. Cover, bring to a boil and simmer for 1 minute. Strain soup and chill thoroughly.
To serve:
In chilled soup bowls garnished with reserved asparagus tips.
To freeze:
This soup freezes well. Use within 2–3 months.
To economize:
Use cooked leeks in place of asparagus.

Mulligatawny Soup

To make: 25 minutes   **To cook:** 1½ hours   **Serves 4–6**

1 lb. neck of lamb
5 cups water
2 onions
2 carrots
1 small apple
salt and pepper
1 tablespoon raisins
2 tablespoons fat or drippings
¼ cup flour
½–1 tablespoon curry powder
1 teaspoon lemon juice
Quick tip:
Use a pressure cooker (see method)
and whirl in a blender.

Put the lamb into a pan with the water, chopped onions and carrots, sliced apple, salt and pepper and raisins. Cover the pan and simmer gently for 1¼ hours. Lift the lamb from the pan and remove the meat from the bones. Sieve or blend the meat and vegetables to give a smooth purée. Heat the fat or drippings, stir in the flour and curry powder then stir in the purée. Bring to a boil, stir over low heat until thickened. Add the lemon juice and salt and pepper to taste.
To serve:
As a hot or cold soup; it is particularly good served cold.
    To serve with Mulligatawny Soup: If cold, top with diced green pepper (discard seeds), finely chopped green onions, flaked coconut or raw cauliflowerets. The same garnishes can also be used for hot soup, together with crisp toasted or fried croûtons of bread.
To vary:
Use less stock and a little light cream or milk.
To freeze:
A good soup for freezing. Use within 2 months.
To economize:
Use up the stock after cooking Spring Lamb, page 71, and omit the pieces of meat.

Chilled Fish Cream

To make: 15 minutes   **To cook:** 15 minutes   **Serves 4–6**

1 small flounder
1 pint water
bouquet garni (see page 28)
salt and pepper
1 can (7 oz.) salmon
few drops Tabasco
juice of ½–1 lemon
⅔ cup light cream
To garnish:
little chopped parsley or fennel leaves
Quick tip:
Use all canned salmon and flavor the
water with anchovy paste.

Have fish filleted and skinned. Put the bones and skin into the water with the bouquet garni and salt and pepper and simmer for 10 minutes, strain and return the fish stock to the pan. Cut the flounder fillets into very small pieces and simmer in the stock for 5 minutes, then add the flaked salmon, salt and pepper and the lemon juice. Chill.
To serve:
Very cold. Beat in the cream just before serving and top with the parsley or fennel.
To vary:
Use prepared shrimp or other shellfish instead of the salmon. Add a very little curry powder to the other ingredients. Sieve or blend the soup with the cream before adding the garnish. Add tiny matchsticks of cucumber and pimiento just before serving.
To freeze:
The soup is better freshly prepared, but frozen fish can be used.
To economize:
Use inexpensive whiting, cod, haddock.

Frosted Tomato Soup

To make: 10 minutes   **To cook:** 5 minutes   **Serves 4**

1¼ cups chicken stock or water and 1 chicken bouillon cube
1 lb. tomatoes, skinned
1 teaspoon Worcestershire sauce
2 teaspoons sherry
salt and pepper
To garnish:
sour cream, chopped chives, chopped parsley

Heat the stock or water and bouillon cube, put in the tomatoes and heat for 1–2 minutes only. Sieve or blend; if you want a very smooth mixture you must sieve to get rid of all the seeds. Add Worcestershire sauce, sherry and salt and pepper. Cool, pour into a freezing tray and freeze until mushy.
To serve:
In chilled soup cups, topped with sour cream and the herbs.
To vary:
Use a generous 2½ cups tomato juice and omit stock and tomatoes.

Watercress Soup

To make: 20 minutes   **To cook:** 20 minutes   **Serves 4**

1 bunch watercress
1 tablespoon oil
2½ cups chicken stock or water and 2 chicken bouillon cubes
2 tablespoons cornstarch
⅔ cup milk
salt and pepper
¼ cup cream, light or heavy
Quick tip:
Sauté watercress as method, add canned condensed cream of chicken soup and dilute with milk. Heat or chill, add cream to taste.

Wash the watercress, reserving some small sprigs to garnish the soup, and chop the remaining leaves coarsely. Sauté slowly for 2–3 minutes in the hot oil. Add the stock or water and bouillon cubes, bring to boiling point, stirring, then simmer for about 15 minutes. Do not overcook as the flavor of the watercress will be lost. Rub through a sieve or whirl in a blender and return to the pan. Mix the cornstarch smoothly with the milk, add to the purée and cook for 3 minutes, stirring well until thick. Add salt and pepper. Just before serving stir in the cream and garnish with sprigs of watercress.
To vary:
This soup is very good made with ham stock.
   Chilled watercress soup: Use only 2 cups chicken stock or water and 2 chicken bouillon cubes. Cook and sieve as the recipe above then chill. Mix with 1¼ cups light cream, a little lemon juice and salt and pepper. Garnish with sprigs of watercress and serve as cold as possible.
To freeze:
Make the watercress purée, freeze this and use within 3–4 months. Add the cornstarch mixture or cream after defrosting and then cook until thick.
To economize:
Omit cream and use extra milk.

Chilled asparagus almond soup

Fish Soups

No soup is more neglected in this country than the fish soup, but these are extremely popular in many Continental countries and many are made with inexpensive fish.

A fish soup is an ideal dish for the elderly or someone who is ill, for you have a meal in a soup bowl which is easy to eat and digest.

The recipes that follow are basic ones that you can adapt by adding additional flavorings such as a pinch of saffron, a few drops of Tabasco or anchovy paste.

Shrimp chowder

Shrimp Chowder

To make: 20 minutes   **To cook:** 30 minutes   **Serves 4**

1 large onion
1 tablespoon butter
⅔ cup boiling water
3 medium-sized potatoes
salt and pepper
1 lb. shrimps, cooked
2½ cups milk
½ cup grated Cheddar cheese
1 tablespoon chopped parsley
Quick tip:
Use 4–6 oz. frozen shelled and deveined shrimps.

Peel, slice and sauté the onion in the butter for 5 minutes until soft but not brown. Add the boiling water, diced potatoes and salt and pepper. Cover and simmer gently for 15–20 minutes, or until the potatoes are just cooked. Add the shelled and deveined shrimps and the milk and reheat. Stir in the grated cheese and parsley.
To serve:
Hot with crusty bread or toast.
To freeze:
Do not freeze this dish, although frozen shrimps could be used.
To economize:
Cook diced white fish fillets with the potatoes, then add a smaller quantity of shrimps.

Spiced Fish Soup

To make: 15 minutes   **To cook:** 25 minutes   Serves 4–6

8 oz. white or smoked fish
1 onion
¼ cup butter or margarine
1 tablespoon flour
good pinch ground cinnamon
good pinch curry powder
3 cups water
1 teaspoon Worcestershire sauce
2 tomatoes
salt and pepper
1–2 slices toast
Quick tip:
Use instant minced onion.

Cut the fish into small pieces, peel and chop the onion. Heat the butter or margarine and sauté the fish and onion in this until golden colored. Stir in the flour, with the cinnamon and curry powder, then stir in the water. Bring to a boil and stir until slightly thickened. Add the Worcestershire sauce, skinned and chopped tomatoes and salt and pepper. Simmer for 10 minutes. Cut the toast into small croûtons.
To serve:
Top the soup with the toast just before serving.
To vary:
Add diced celery and pepper (discard core and seeds) with the tomatoes.
To freeze:
This soup freezes well. Use within 1 month.
To economize:
Choose the least expensive fish.

Salmon Bisque

To make: 15 minutes   **To cook:** 20 minutes   Serves 4–6

1 lemon
1 onion
3¾ cups milk
¼ cup butter or margarine
½ cup flour
8 oz. cooked or canned salmon
salt and pepper
¼–⅓ cup light cream
To garnish:
little cucumber
Quick tip:
Use a little instant minced onion and canned salmon.

Peel rind from the lemon; do not use any of the bitter white part, just the colored part. Peel the onion and halve. Put the lemon rind and onion into the milk, bring the milk to boiling point, then strain. Heat the butter or margarine, stir in the flour, then gradually stir in the strained milk. Stir over moderate heat until thickened, add the flaked salmon, salt and pepper and cream. Heat gently, but do not boil. Add a very little juice from the lemon and season to taste.
To serve:
Pour into hot soup cups and top with matchstick pieces of cucumber.
To vary:
Use any other fish in place of salmon.
To freeze:
This is not a good soup to freeze, but is an ideal way of using frozen salmon.
To economize:
Use canned pink salmon.

Smoked Haddock Broth

To make: 15 minutes   **To cook:** 25 minutes   Serves 4–6

1 small piece smoked haddock, about 1 lb.
1–2 onions
2½ cups milk
1¼ cups water
pepper
1 tablespoon long-grain rice
1–2 eggs
To garnish:
1 tablespoon chopped parsley
Quick tip:
Use fillets of smoked haddock which are quicker to flake, and instant minced onion.

Cut the haddock into 4 portions. Peel and chop the onion(s). Put the fish and onion(s) into the milk and water with pepper to taste. Poach for about 10 minutes, or until the fish is cooked. Remove fish from the liquid and flake finely. Meanwhile add the rice and simmer until soft. Hard-cook, shell and chop the egg(s). Add the fish and egg(s) to the soup and heat for 2–3 minutes only.
To serve:
Top with parsley.
To vary:
Use smoked white fish instead of smoked haddock and add a pinch of saffron powder to the liquid. Skin and bone white fish and break into large chunks. Stir a little cream into the soup before serving.
To freeze:
This freezes moderately well. I would only freeze to prevent any soup from being wasted. Use within 3–4 weeks.
To economize:
Use cheaper smoked white fish (see To vary) and add salt to the milk.

Garnishes for Soups

Soups look more interesting garnished with chopped herbs or tiny fried or toasted diced bread (known as croûtons). Yogurt, cream or chopped nuts are nourishing toppings.

Meat Soups

The stock from cooking meat is particularly good to give a definite flavor to a soup, but in addition there are many soups based upon meat. Some of the most practical ones are given on these two pages.

The recipes can also be adapted to use other meats, for example the recipe for Turkey Purée Soup could be followed with beef, lamb or veal bones, or a game carcass, using any meat on the bone. The Chicken Consommé with Meat Dumplings is equally as good with beef, using beef bones instead of chicken bones.

Oxtail soup:

A recipe for cooking oxtail is given on page 81. Generally there is quite an amount of liquid left over in this recipe as one must cover the pieces of oxtail to prevent them from drying. I put this, plus any vegetables left, into the blender or through a sieve to give a thick soup. If, however, you want to make a thinner soup, follow the recipe for cooking oxtail on page 81, but use only half the amount of meat and vegetables then sieve or blend.

Kidney and bacon soup

Kidney & Bacon Soup

To make: 20 minutes   **To cook:** 1½ hours   **Serves 4–6**

8 oz. beef kidney
2 onions
2 slices bacon
2 tablespoons fat or beef drippings
3 cups beef stock or water and 3 beef
    bouillon cubes
salt and pepper
1 tablespoon flour
1 carrot (optional)

Chop kidney, peel onions and dice bacon. Fry the bacon until the bacon is crisp. Remove crisp bacon pieces. Heat the fat or drippings and sauté the kidney and onions in this for 5 minutes. Add most of the stock, or water and bouillon cubes, with salt and pepper. Cover the pan and simmer gently for 1 hour. Mix the flour with the remaining stock, stir into the soup and cook until slightly thickened. Scrape and grate the carrot, add to the soup and cook for 5 minutes (this could be omitted).

To serve:
Topped with the crisp bacon.

To freeze:
This freezes well, use within 6 weeks.

To economize:
Use bacon or ham pieces.

Chicken Consommé with Herb Dumplings

To make: 30 minutes   **To cook:** 2¼ hours   **Serves 6–8**

1 chicken carcass
water
bouquet garni (see page 28)
salt and pepper
2 chicken bouillon cubes (see method)
2 cups chopped mixed vegetables
2 tomatoes
1–2 tablespoons chopped parsley
For the dumplings:
½ cup self-rising flour (or all-purpose
    flour with ½ teaspoon baking
    powder)
pinch salt
2 tablespoons ground beef suet
¼–½ tablespoon chopped chives
¼–½ tablespoon chopped parsley
water to mix
Quick tip:
Use water and bouillon cubes with
frozen vegetables.

Put chicken carcass into a large saucepan with water to cover. Add the bouquet garni and salt and pepper; bouillon cubes can be added for extra flavor later. Simmer for 2 hours then strain the liquid. Return this to the pan. Any chicken could be removed from the bones, diced and added with the tomatoes. Prepare and dice the vegetables. Add to the stock and bring to a boil. Sift the flour or flour and baking powder with the salt. Add suet, herbs and enough water to make a soft dough. Roll into tiny balls (the size of a hazelnut) with floured fingers and drop into the boiling liquid. Cook for 10 minutes then add the skinned, finely chopped tomatoes and parsley and heat for a further 5 minutes. Serve hot.

To vary:
Beef bones or other poultry could be used.

To freeze:
This soup, plus the dumplings, freezes well. Use within 2 months.

To economize:
This is an excellent way of using the carcass of a roasted chicken which is so often wasted.

Turkey Purée Soup

To make: 30 minutes   **To cook:** 1–3 hours   **Serves about 8**

1 turkey carcass, left from roast turkey
water
salt and pepper
vegetables to taste, e.g. onions,
    carrots, turnips
heavy or light cream
Quick tip:
Use a pressure cooker (see method).

Put the turkey carcass into a large pan with water to cover, salt and pepper and vegetables. Simmer the liquid for 2–3 hours then lift the bones from the liquid. Cool sufficiently to handle, then take all the tiny pieces of meat from the bones. Sieve the meat or blend with some of the stock. Purée the cooked vegetables as well. To save cooking time use a pressure cooker at 15 lb. pressure for about 30 minutes, see page 11. Put the turkey and vegetable purées into a pan and dilute with enough stock to make the consistency of light cream. Any stock left over can be used in cooking, or see Chicken Consommé above. Heat with any extra salt and pepper required.

To serve:
Top each portion with a little cream.

To freeze:
An excellent soup for freezing. Use within 2–3 months.

Fish

We are very fortunate in having a wide choice of fish and most of this can be cooked in a variety of ways, as the following pages show.

The basic methods of cooking are all given in this section together with newer ideas to give a pleasant change to fish cooking.

As fish has a delicate taste you can make the dish more interesting by the wise use of herbs and sauces. Some of the best herbs to use with fish are fennel, dill and tarragon as well as the better known parsley.

Whatever method you select there is one golden rule — never over-cook fish, as it loses its moist texture and much of its flavor.

Check carefully when you buy fish to make sure it is really fresh. It should smell pleasant, with no trace of the odor of ammonia, the scales and eyes should be bright, and the fish feel firm.

Avoid buying fish when they are not in season, for this means they tend to be very "watery" and have large roes, so there is very little flesh to cook. Check the weight of crab and lobster by the size of the fish. If they feel surprisingly light they are "watery" and poor value.

Economical fish dishes: There are a number of inexpensive dishes in this section, but one way to save money is to choose fish that is plentiful and cheaper. Buy frozen fish when fresh fish is not available.

There is also a good range of frozen fish available today; store this as directed on the package. You will find that most frozen fish does not need defrosting and can be cooked from the frozen state. Hints on freezing fish dishes are given under the recipes, and on page 48.

To fry fish: One of the best and most popular ways to cook fish is to fry it. The coating of flour or flour plus beaten egg and crumbs or batter keeps the fish moist, while allowing the outside to become crisp and brown. The method of coating with batter is on page 44, and this is particularly suitable for deep frying.

To coat fish with egg and crumbs: Dry the fish, then coat in a little flour seasoned with salt and pepper. Beat an egg with a little water, then brush this over the fish. Coat in fine dry breadcrumbs. The easiest and tidiest way to coat the fish is either to put the crumbs on a sheet of wax paper and lay the fish on this, pressing the crumbs firmly against both sides of the fish with a broad-bladed knife, or to put the crumbs into a large plastic bag, drop the fish into the bag and shake vigorously until the fish is coated.

The only drawback in using a bag for coating fish is that you tend to spoil the shape of rather large fillets, so I would reserve this method for smaller pieces of fish or fairly substantial cutlets or portions which will retain their original appearance.

Secrets of good shallow frying: Heat a little oil or fat in a large frying pan. Make sure this is hot then put in the coated fish. Fry quickly until crisp and brown, turn and fry quickly on the second side. Thin fillets of fish take only about 4 minutes on each side. Thicker fish cutlets or whole fish need about 8 minutes, so lower the heat and complete cooking more slowly. Drain on absorbent paper and serve with lemon, tartar sauce, page 55, and fried potatoes, page 104.

Frying fish

Fish and bacon whirls

To coat fish in batter

If you prefer to deep fry fish, you may coat in egg and crumbs, as page 42, or in batter.

To coat 4–6 portions of fish
Sift 1 cup all-purpose or self-rising flour with a pinch of salt. Beat in 1 egg and ⅔ cup milk, to give a fairly thick batter. This is ideal for solid portions of fish, see opposite, but to coat thin fillets of fish or scampi, add ⅓ cup extra milk or water to give a more delicate coating. Coat the fish with seasoned flour, then batter.

Secrets of Deep Frying

Half-fill a deep fat fryer with oil or fat, with the frying basket in position. Heat the oil or fat carefully, then test with a cube of day-old bread. It should turn golden in under 1 minute.

Place the coated fish into the basket and fry, allowing about 3 minutes for fillets or scampi, 6–7 minutes for thicker portions.

Lift out the basket slowly, so the oil or fat drains back into the pan. Drain the fish on absorbent paper and serve as shallow fried fish, page 42.

Fish to fry

Most fish can be fried, either in shallow or in deep fat. Here are some of the best fish to fry and methods of coating.

White fish:
Cod, haddock, turbot, flounder, sole: Coat in egg and crumbs or batter and shallow or deep fry as pages 42 or 44. The more luxurious sole is also delicious cooked as Fish Meunière, below.

Oily fish:
Smelts, mackerel, trout, salmon: Coat in seasoned flour or seasoned cornmeal and shallow fry. Trout can be cooked as Fish Meunière, opposite.

44

Shellfish:

Large shrimp, known as scampi, can be coated in seasoned flour, then egg and crumbs or a thin coating of batter. While they can be shallow fried, they are nicer cooked in deep oil or fat, see above. Oysters, clams or prawns can be prepared and fried in the same way. Do not over-cook shellfish.

Fish cakes:

Mix equal quantities of mashed potatoes and flaked cooked fish, season with salt and pepper and flavor with chopped parsley. Add egg to bind and form into round hamburger-shaped cakes. Coat in seasoned flour, egg and crumbs and shallow fry as page 42.

Fish & Bacon Whirls

To make: 10 minutes   **To cook:** 10 minutes   **Serves 4**

1½ lbs. fillet of haddock, cod, halibut, cut into 4 pieces
1 tablespoon flour
salt and pepper
1 egg
1 cup dry breadcrumbs
4 slices bacon
4 tomatoes
To fry:
little oil or fat
Quick tip:
Buy frozen breaded portions of fish and fry from frozen state.

Dry the fish and coat in the flour, mixed with the salt and pepper, then in beaten egg and crumbs. Fry in hot oil or fat until nearly cooked (approximately 4–5 minutes for thin fillets and 6–7 minutes for thicker pieces). Remove from the frying pan and place on a plate. Cut each slice of bacon in half lengthwise and twist around the portions of fish. Fasten with toothpicks. Return the fish to the frying pan with halved seasoned tomatoes and cook for a further 2–3 minutes, turning once, so the bacon becomes crisp.
To serve:
Hot with a green vegetable or salad.
To vary:
Use whole smelts. Remove heads. Coat in seasoned flour, but omit the egg and crumbs. Fry as above or broil if preferred.
To freeze:
Although you can use frozen fish, it is better to prepare and freeze, rather than cook and freeze, as this dish is better served immediately after cooking.
To economize:
Use the most inexpensive fish such as turbot, pollack.

Fish Meunière

To make: 10 minutes   **To cook:** 6–12 minutes   **Serves 4**

4 portions white fish (sole, turbot, etc.) or fresh shrimp or scallops (about 1½ lbs.)
salt and pepper
½ cup butter
½–1 tablespoon lemon juice
½–1 tablespoon chopped parsley
1–2 teaspoons capers

Sprinkle the fish with salt and pepper. Fry in the hot butter until cooked, then remove from the pan and keep hot. Heat butter remaining in pan until golden, add lemon juice, parsley and capers and heat for 1–2 minutes.
To serve:
Spoon the butter mixture over the fish.
To vary:
Fish in Riesling cream: Fry the fish as above, allow the butter to turn golden, then add ½ cup Riesling and ½ cup light cream, heat without boiling, add parsley and capers and serve.
To freeze:
Do not freeze the cooked dish, but frozen fish can be used. Cook without defrosting it first.
To economize:
Use vinegar instead of lemon juice.

Trout with Almonds

To make: 10 minutes   **To cook:** 10 minutes   **Serves 4**

4 large trout
1 tablespoon flour
salt and pepper
6 tablespoons butter
⅓ cup blanched slivered almonds
2 teaspoons lemon juice
To garnish:
watercress

If using frozen trout there is no need to defrost these. Mix the flour and salt and pepper, coat the fish with this and fry in the hot butter until just cooked. Add the almonds during cooking and fry these with the fish. Lift the fish and nuts on to a hot dish. Heat the lemon juice with drippings in the pan, spoon over the fish and serve at once, garnished with watercress.
To vary:
Use fillets of sole or portions of turbot or see "To economize".
To freeze:
Cook lightly, freeze, reheat for a short time. Use within 1 month.
To economize:
Use filleted mackerel.

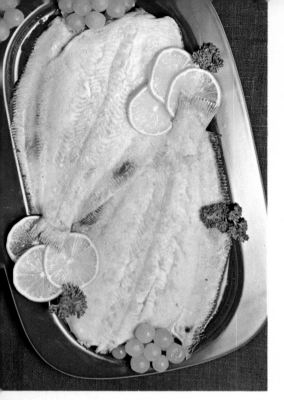

Sole and grapes

To Broil Fish

Many of the fish that can be fried are equally as good when broiled. In addition to the fish listed on page 44 you can broil kippers.

Secrets of broiling fish:
Always preheat the broiler before putting the fish underneath; this makes certain it cooks quickly and does not dry.

Brush the fish with melted butter or oil before and during cooking. It is also advisable to oil the rack of the broiler pan before putting on the fish; this prevents the fish sticking.

Season the fish, with salt and pepper, add a little lemon juice or chopped herbs to the butter or oil, then coat the fish. Cook thin fillets of fish for 4–5 minutes without turning. Turn thicker pieces of fish and lower the heat after both sides are golden colored.

Flounder with mushrooms and tomatoes
Put halved tomatoes and mushroom caps seasoned with salt and pepper on the rack of the broiler pan with the fish. Brush with melted butter and broil quickly.

Sole and grapes
Broil whole sole and when nearly cooked add peeled grapes coated with melted butter and heat for 1–2 minutes only. Garnish with parsley and lemon slices.

Moules au Gratin

To make: 15 minutes   **To cook:** 12 minutes   **Serves 4**

2 quarts mussels (prepared and cooked as page 48)
5 tablespoons butter
6 tablespoons flour
wine from preparing mussels
¼ cup light cream
⅓ cup grated Parmesan cheese
⅓ cup dry breadcrumbs

Prepare the mussels as method under Moules Americaine (page 48); strain and save the wine. Heat 3 tablespoons of the butter in a pan, stir in the flour and cook for several minutes. Gradually stir in nearly 2 cups of cooking liquid. Bring the sauce to a boil, stirring well, and cook until thickened over low heat; add mussels and heat for 2–3 minutes. Remove from the heat and stir in the cream. Spoon into a flameproof dish, top with the cheese and crumbs, dot with remaining butter and brown under the broiler for a few minutes.
To serve:
As soon as cooked, as an hors d'oeuvre or main dish.
To economize:
Use hard cider in sauce (see page 48) instead of wine.

Norfolk Herrings

To make: 15 minutes   **To cook:** 10 minutes   **Serves 4**

4 large fresh herrings
6 tablespoons butter or margarine
1 tablespoons prepared mustard
1 large onion
salt and pepper
1 tablespoon chopped parsley
To garnish:
lemon, watercress
Quick tip:
Top whiting fillets with the flavored butter in the recipe, broil for 2–3 minutes.

Have the herrings boned and filleted. Save the roes and chop finely. To bone herring at home, insert the knife into the herrings and cut into the fish towards the center until they can be opened out flat. Lay the cut side downwards on to a board, run your finger firmly down the center backbone, then turn over again and lift away the bones. Cream 4 tablespoons of the butter or margarine with the chopped roes, mustard, grated onion, salt and pepper and parsley. Spread over the inside of the herrings. Place under a preheated broiler and cook for 4–5 minutes. Remove from the heat, fold the herrings over and brush with the remaining butter which should be melted and mixed with salt and pepper. Continue to broil until cooked.
To serve:
With wedges of lemon and watercress. These are also very good when cooked and served cold.
To freeze:
Prepare, but do not cook, wrap and freeze. Use within 6 weeks.
To economize:
Mix soft breadcrumbs with the filling to make it go further.

Broiled flounder with mushrooms and tomatoes

To Freeze Fish:

Many people are avid fishermen and are therefore able to obtain fairly large quantities of fish. It is well worth freezing any that cannot be cooked at that time. Fish must be very fresh to freeze well.

Prepare the fish, cut into convenient-sized portions, separate fillets, etc. Wrap well. Use white fish within 6 months; oily fish (salmon, mackerel, etc.) within 4 months and shellfish within 2 months. See page 52 for freezing smoked fish.

Secrets of Poaching Fish:

Poaching fish is often described as "boiling" but this term really is incorrect as fish that is boiled rapidly is spoiled in both texture and flavor. The liquid should simmer gently. Fish can be poached just in salt and pepper seasoned water; in water flavored with lemon juice with a sliced carrot and sliced onion; in white wine or cider; in fish stock (this is made by simmering fish, skin and bones in seasoned water); or in a court bouillon. To make this, mix equal quantities of white wine and water, add a bay leaf and any other herbs you like (e.g. fennel, dill, thyme) and a carrot and onion. The fish can be placed into cold liquid to cover; this is then brought to simmering point. If using this method shorten the times given below by 2–3 minutes in each case. If preferred, bring the liquid to simmering point, add the fish and time as follows:

Allow 7 minutes per pound for fillets of fish or thin steaks or 10 minutes per pound for whole fish or large portions.

If cooking small portions to serve cold, follow the method for poaching salmon steaks below.

To Poach Salmon Steaks:

Large pieces of salmon or the whole fish should be cooked as above, allowing 10 minutes per pound, but making sure water just simmers. Salmon steaks can be cooked in the same way, but I find a better method as follows:

Make a large square of foil for each portion of fish or use a plastic cooking bag. Butter the paper or bag well. Lay the fish on this, season and flavor with lemon juice, salt and pepper and a little butter or oil. Seal the foil or bag. Put into cold water, bring this to boiling point slowly. Remove from the heat when the water comes to a boil, cover well, leave fish in the water until cold.

If serving hot, follow timing under poaching.

°Moules Américaine

To make: 30 minutes   **To cook:** 20 minutes   **Serves 4–6**

2½ quarts mussels
1¼ cups white wine
⅔ cup water
salt and pepper
bunch parsley
1 lb. tomatoes
little chopped parsley
little chopped basil
Quick tip:
Heat canned whole clams in wine and tomato mixture.

Scrub the mussels thoroughly, discard any that do not close when tapped sharply; this is very important, as it could mean that the fish has been dead for some time. Remove black strings on outside of shell. Put into a large heavy pan with the wine, water, salt and pepper and bunch of parsley. Cook over medium heat for 6–8 minutes until the shells are open; discard any that remain closed. Cool slightly, remove the mussels from the shells. Meanwhile slice the tomatoes (skin if wished) and add to the liquid in the pan. Simmer for about 10 minutes, remove the bunch of parsley and add the chopped herbs and a little more salt and pepper. Put the mussels into the liquid and heat for 1 minute only.
To serve:
With green salad and French bread. A good hors d'oeuvre or main dish.
To freeze:
Freeze for 2–3 weeks only; heat gently to serve.
To economize:
Use hard cider in place of wine.

Coquilles St. Jacques

Coquilles St. Jacques

To make: 15 minutes   **To cook:** 25–30 minutes   **Serves 3–6**

1 lb. large scallops
2 cups milk
salt and pepper
1 lb. peeled potatoes
6 tablespoons butter
little light cream or milk (see method)
½ cup flour
To garnish:
lemon, parsley
Quick tip:
Use condensed cream of mushroom
soup instead of making the sauce.

Put scallops into the pan with the milk and a little salt and pepper. Simmer steadily for just 10 minutes, no longer. Meanwhile cook the potatoes in boiling salted water, drain, then mash with 2 tablespoons of the butter and a very little cream or milk. Melt the remaining butter in a pan, stir in the flour, cook gently for 2–3 minutes, then stir in the strained liquid from cooking the scallops. Bring the sauce to a boil, stir over low heat until thickened. Add scallops and spoon into shells or small individual casseroles. Put the potatoes into a pastry bag with a 1/2-inch star tip and pipe a border around the edge of the shells, brown for a few minutes under a broiler. Garnish with lemon and parsley.

To serve:
Hot as an hors d'oeuvre or a main course; serve two scallops for a main dish.

To vary:
Coquilles St. Jacques Mornay: Make the recipe as above, heat the scallops in the sauce then add ½ cup finely grated Swiss or Gruyère cheese and ½ cup sliced sautéed mushrooms, heat gently, then put into the shells as above. This recipe is shown in the picture above.

Scallops and Bacon: Wrap each well seasoned scallop in bacon, secure with toothpicks and broil until bacon is crisp on all sides.

Scallop Fritters: Make the coating batter on page 44, using only the ⅔ cup milk. Coat about 1 lb. large scallops in the batter and deep fry for 5–6 minutes. Serve with tartar sauce, page 55.

To freeze:
The basic recipe and variation with cheese freeze well; use within 1 month.

To economize:
Use diced white fish with fewer scallops.

49

Secrets of
Baking Fish

Remember when baking fish that it must not be spoiled by over-cooking, so that ingredients added, e.g. onions, must be grated or thinly sliced, so they do not prolong the cooking time.

To prepare:

The simplest way to bake fish is to put it into a buttered dish, season with salt and pepper and flavor it with lemon juice and top with melted butter and/or milk. For a golden top leave the dish uncovered, for a moist topping, cover the dish. Allow a few minutes longer cooking time when covering the dish. Bake for 12–20 minutes (depending upon the thickness of the fish) for fillets in a moderately hot oven, 400°F. Thicker steaks need up to 20–25 minutes, and whole fish about 12 minutes per pound. When you add a number of other ingredients, the temperature and cooking time will need to be adjusted.

Fish Pie

To make: 30 minutes   **To cook:** 50 minutes   **Serves 4–6**

1 lb. peeled potatoes
salt and pepper
1½ lbs. white fish
2 cups white sauce (page 54)
2 tablespoons butter
little milk (see method)

Quick tip:

Use condensed cream of mushroom or other suitable soup instead of making the sauce. Keep all the ingredients hot and brown under the broiler instead of in the oven.

Cook the potatoes in salted water and poach the fish in water seasoned with salt and pepper as page 48. Strain the fish stock and blend with the sauce. Put fish into an ovenproof dish and cover with sauce. Mash the potatoes with butter and a little milk. Spread thinly over the fish mixture and bake in a moderate oven, 375°F. for 25–30 minutes.

To serve:

With baked tomatoes and other vegetables.

To vary:

The above is a very basic recipe that can be varied in many ways:

Cheese Fish Pie: Add grated cheese to the sauce and mashed potatoes.

Add sliced sautéed mushrooms, parsley, sliced hard-cooked eggs to the sauce or mix with diced cooked vegetables.

Bacony Fish Pie: Fry chopped bacon. Place bacon and sliced tomatoes at the bottom of the dish, top with the fish and sauce and potatoes and heat as above.

To freeze:

A fish pie freezes well, except when hard-cooked eggs are added to the sauce. Use within 1 month, heat very gently from the frozen state or thaw out and then heat.

To economize:

Use some fish stock in the sauce and the least expensive fish. Use more potatoes for topping.

Psari Plaki

To make: 20–25 minutes   **To cook:** 1¼ hours   **Serves 4**

4 small mackerel
salt and pepper
juice of ½ a lemon
2 onions
1 lb. potatoes
2 carrots
2 sticks celery
8 oz. tomatoes
3–4 tablespoons olive oil

To garnish:
1 tablespoon chopped parsley

Quick tip:

Use canned mixed vegetables. Drain, season with salt and pepper and put into the casserole with the fish. Top with 2 teaspoons oil, cover and heat for 30 minutes.

This is an interesting way to make a main meal of oily fish. Prepare the fish, i.e. remove the backbones and cut into two fillets, see page 46. Place in a greased ovenproof dish, sprinkle with salt and pepper and the lemon juice. Prepare and thinly slice the vegetables, sauté in the hot oil separately in the following order, onions, potatoes, carrots, celery and tomatoes. Arrange the vegetables around the fish. Cover with greased foil and bake in a moderate oven, 350°F. for 1 hour.

To serve:

Hot, sprinkled with parsley, with a green vegetable.

To vary:

Use mullet or trout instead of mackerel.

To freeze:

Cook as the recipe, but do not over-cook. Cool, cover and freeze. Use within 2–3 weeks. Thaw out, then reheat.

To economize:

Choose mackerel as the basic recipe, for these are one of the cheapest fish.

Psari plaki

Pickled & Smoked Fish

While one can buy pickled herrings it is very easy to prepare your own pickled fish. White fish is excellent cooked in this way, see below.

There are home smoking outfits available now so if you are an avid fisherman and obtain large stocks of mackerel, herrings or salmon you could smoke them yourself; otherwise it means buying the fish ready-smoked. This method of preparing the various fish means they keep rather longer than fresh fish, but do not store for more than a few days except in the freezer. Smoked salmon and other smoked fish keep in good condition in the freezer for up to 6 weeks; separate the slices or portions with freezer paper or foil. Smoked kippers or haddock should be packed in plastic cooking bags, with a piece of butter, and they can be cooked from the frozen state in the bag, so retaining their flavor.

Pickled Fish

To make: 15 minutes   **To cook:** 1 hour   **Serves 4–6**

4–6 portions white fish or herrings,
    mackerel, etc.
2 onions
1–2 bay leaves
1 teaspoon pickling spices
salt and pepper
about 1¼ cups vinegar
water (see method)
To garnish:
salad greens
Quick tip:
Cook for 20 minutes in a covered saucepan.

Place the fish in a dish, add the sliced onions and the rest of the ingredients, except the salad greens. If the vinegar does not cover the fish, add more or dilute with a little water. Cover the dish and bake for 1 hour in slow oven, 300°F.
To serve:
Hot or cold with salad greens; allow to cool in the liquid. Strain the vinegar and use in a dressing for the salad greens.
To vary:
Pickled Herrings: Follow the recipe above, but add a peeled and cored sliced apple, ½–1 teaspoon mixed spice and ½–1 teaspoon sugar to the vinegar liquid. Bone each herring, as page 46, cut into two fillets, then roll each fillet from the head to the tail. Some of the sliced onion can be spread over each fillet before rolling. Fasten with toothpicks. Cook as above.
To freeze:
Although pickled fish can be frozen, some of the flavor tends to be lost. Use within 2–3 weeks.
To economize:
Use cheaper fish, for the pickling improves the flavor.

Kedgeree

To make: 20 minutes   **To cook:** 30 minutes   **Serves 4**

1 medium-sized smoked haddock or
    1 lb. haddock fillet
water
salt and pepper
½ cup long grain rice
2 eggs
¼ cup butter
little milk or cream (see method)
To garnish:
1–2 tablespoons chopped parsley

Cut the haddock into portions, discard tail and fins from the whole fish. Poach in water with pepper to season for about 10 minutes; do not overcook. Cook the rice in another pan in 1½ cups boiling water and a very little salt. Cover the pan and simmer gently for 15 minutes. Meanwhile, hard-cook the eggs and shell. Drain the haddock, flake the fish and discard any bones. Heat the butter in a pan, add the cooked rice (all the liquid should have been absorbed by the end of the cooking time), the fish and enough milk or cream to make a creamy consistency. Heat gently for a few minutes, season with salt and pepper. Chop the egg whites and yolks separately; stir the whites into the fish mixture. Pile on a hot dish and garnish with the chopped egg yolks and parsley.
To serve:
Hot as a supper or breakfast dish with crisp toast.
To vary:
To make a more savory dish, top with fried onion rings.
To freeze:
This dish should be eaten when freshly made but frozen fish could be used.

Smoked Haddock & Cheese Flan

To make: 30 minutes **To cook:** 1 hour **Serves 4–6**

For the flan case:
1¼ cups all-purpose flour
pinch of salt
6 tablespoons butter or margarine
1 egg yolk
water to bind; about 3 tablespoons

For the filling:
8 oz. smoked haddock
⅔ cup water
juice of ½ a lemon
2 tablespoons butter
1 small onion
1 cup sliced mushrooms
2 eggs
½ cup light cream
½ cup cottage cheese
1 tablespoon chopped parsley
salt and pepper

Quick tip:
Use frozen pastry or pie crust mix and canned tuna or salmon in place of haddock. Use an 8 inch pie pan.

Sift the flour and the salt together. Rub the butter into the flour with your fingertips, until the mixture looks like fine breadcrumbs. Add the egg yolk and water to bind the dough. Knead lightly for a few seconds to give a firm, smooth dough. Wrap and chill for 15 minutes. Roll out the pastry to ¼-inch thickness and use to line an 8-inch flan ring on a cookie sheet. Prick the bottom and fill with rice or beans and bake in a moderately hot oven, 400°F. for 15 minutes. Remove beans or rice and continue baking for a further 5–10 minutes until the pastry is lightly browned. Cool. Poach the haddock in a pan with the water and half the lemon juice. Drain, discard the skin and bones and flake the fish. Melt the butter in a pan, cook the finely chopped onion for a few minutes then add the chopped mushrooms and continue cooking for 3–4 minutes. Mix the fish and vegetables and spread evenly in baked shell. Beat the eggs with the cream, cheese, remaining lemon juice and parsley. Season with salt and pepper lightly. Pour over the fish mixture. Bake in a moderate oven, 350–375°F. for 30–35 minutes until set and golden.

To serve:
Hot or cold with a salad or vegetables or by itself.

To freeze:
This freezes excellently. In this case it is better to cook, then freeze the complete dish. Wrap after freezing. Use within 6 weeks. Reheat gently from the frozen state.

To economize:
Use milk in place of cream and an inexpensive white fish or flaked cooked kippers in place of smoked haddock. Use left-over dry cheese in place of cottage cheese; grate this finely.

Smoked haddock and cheese flan

Sauces for Fish

Many fish dishes are improved by the addition of a sauce and this can turn simple poached or broiled fish into unusual and interesting dishes.

White sauce: This is a basic sauce upon which so many other sauces are based. The proportions given here produce a coating sauce, ideal to serve over, or with fish. The version opposite gives a thick sauce, used to bind ingredients together.

To make a coating sauce: Heat 2 tablespoons butter or margarine in a pan, stir in either ¼ cup flour or 2 tablespoons cornstarch. Cook for several minutes, stirring well. Gradually stir in 1¼ cups milk, bring to a boil and cook over medium heat until thickened. Stir as the sauce thickens and allow it to simmer gently for several minutes. Season to taste with salt and pepper.
To freeze: This sauce or dishes containing this and similar sauces, use cornstarch rather than flour, as it makes a sauce that is less likely to curdle. If the sauce does curdle (separate) slightly, beat with whisk or whirl in the blender before heating.

Anchovy sauce: Add a few drops of anchovy paste or several finely chopped anchovy fillets to the white sauce.

Béchamel sauce: Warm the milk with a piece of onion, carrot, celery and a bay leaf. Stand for a time then use (after straining) in the white sauce, above.

Cheese sauce: Make the sauce above, then add 1 cup (4 oz.) grated Cheddar cheese; do not cook the sauce again after adding the cheese.

Curry sauce: A creamed curry sauce is delicious with white fish. Make the white sauce, adding ½–1 tablespoon curry powder with the flour. When the sauce has thickened, remove from the heat, beat in ⅓ cup light or heavy cream and serve.

Cold curry sauce: To serve with fish salads is made by adding a little curry powder and whipped cream to mayonnaise, page 111.

Fennel sauce: Fennel leaves give a delicious flavor to fish. Chop finely and add 2–3 teaspoons to the white sauce above. Fennel mayonnaise is made by adding the chopped fennel to mayonnaise, see page 111. More sauces are given on page 82.

Fish in a jacket

Fish in a Jacket

To make: 35 minutes   **To bake:** 35 minutes   **Serves 4–6**

1 lb. frozen puff pastry or puff pastry
    made with 2 cups all-purpose flour,
    etc. (see page 97)
4 very large or 6 smaller fillets white
    fish
salt and pepper
For the sauce:
2 tablespoons butter
¼ cup flour
⅔ cup milk
4 oz. mushrooms
salt and pepper
To glaze:
1 egg
1 tablespoon water
To garnish:
lemon
parsley
Quick tip:
Use frozen puff pastry and 5–6
tablespoons well seasoned heavy
cream in place of white sauce.

Thaw frozen pastry or prepare the pastry and roll out thinly on a floured surface. Cut into 4 or 6 squares, large enough to cover the fish. Lay the fillets flat on a board and season lightly with salt and pepper. Make a thick sauce with the butter, flour and milk, see opposite. Add the chopped uncooked mushrooms and season with salt and pepper. Spread sauce over half of each fillet. Fold the other half of the fish over the sauce. Lay on the squares of pastry, moisten the edges with water, fold over in triangles and seal the edges. Lift on to a baking sheet, brush with a little beaten egg, blended with water. Bake for 10 minutes in a very hot oven, 475°F. then lower the heat to moderate, 350–375°F. and bake for a further 20–25 minutes until golden brown and well risen. Garnish with lemon and parsley.

To serve:
Hot or cold with a green salad.

To vary:
If preferred, mix flaked cooked fish with a thick white sauce and chopped mushrooms and use as a filling for the pastry.

   Fish crêpes: The filling given in the variation above makes a good filling for crêpes. Make and cook crêpes as page 137. Cook and flake the fish, mix with the thick white sauce and sliced sautéed mushrooms. Spread over the crêpes, roll and serve. For a more moist dish make an additional coating sauce, put some in an ovenproof dish, add the filled crêpes, top with more sauce and bake in a moderate oven, 350°F. for 25–30 minutes.

To freeze:
It is better to prepare the fish triangles, freeze then wrap. Use within 4–6 weeks. Allow to defrost then cook as recipe. If you cook the triangles and freeze after cooking, heat gently from the frozen state. The fish crêpes freeze well, use within 1 month.

To economize:
See To vary.

Tartar Sauce

To make: 10 minutes   **No cooking**   **Serves 4**

⅔ cup mayonnaise (see page 111)
½–1 tablespoon chopped gherkins
½–1 tablespoons chopped parsley
1–2 teaspoons capers

Mix all the ingredients together. This sauce is excellent with fried or broiled fish.

To vary:
Add other chopped herbs, including chopped fennel.

To freeze:
Do not freeze as this sauce tends to curdle.

Cod with Green Sauce

To make: 15 minutes   **To cook:** 15 minutes   **Serves 4**

1 medium-sized onion
3 tablespoons chopped parsley
2 teaspoons capers
2–3 gherkins
½ a 2 oz. can anchovy fillets
1 tablespoon soft breadcrumbs
1 tablespoon olive oil
juice of 1 lemon
salt and pepper
4 steaks or pieces white fish (cod,
    halibut or haddock), about 1½ lbs.
Quick tip:
Put all the ingredients for the sauce
into the blender, whirl for 30 seconds.

Grate the onion and pound in a mortar together with the parsley, capers, chopped gherkins and anchovies. Continue pounding until a smooth paste is achieved, add the breadcrumbs and continue to pound. Pour in the oil and mix well, then add the lemon juice and season with pepper, and salt if necessary. Put the fish into an ovenproof dish, season with salt and pepper and cover each piece of fish with sauce. Cover the dish and bake for approximately 15 minutes in a moderately hot oven, 400°F.

To serve:
With boiled or baked potatoes.

To vary:
Cod with red sauce: Omit anchovies and parsley and add skinned, chopped tomatoes.

To freeze:
Do not freeze this dish, but you can use frozen fish portions.

To economize:
Omit the anchovies.

Meat

Cooking meat: Meat is one of the more important foods in most family budgets, so buy wisely and learn to select the right cut for each cooking method. Store in the refrigerator, or cook soon after purchase. When buying look for the following points:

Beef: bright, moist-looking red lean with some fat, which should be firm and white.

Lamb: firm, pale pink lean, creamy-white fat; mutton is darker in color with more fat.

Pork: pale pink lean, firm white fat.

Veal: very pale pink lean, very little fat.

Economical meat dishes: There are a number of inexpensive meat dishes in this section, see page 76 onwards.

Stuffings and pastry can play an important part increasing the flavor of meat dishes and also help to economize by making meat go further. Do not be too conservative in your choice of stuffings. Recipes are given under various meat and poultry dishes, but these can be adapted in many ways. Use different herbs, add fruits and nuts for new flavors and textures.

Take the recipe on page 83 for a veal (parsley and thyme) stuffing as a basic recipe and enjoy changing this; for example you can add chopped mint in place of parsley as a stuffing with lamb; chives plus sage instead of parsley for a new stuffing with pork and duck; a little grated fresh horseradish and rather less parsley to serve with beef. Add chopped cooked apricots or prunes or chopped raw apples or plums to the same basic stuffing; these blend particularly well with rich meats or game. Chopped walnuts, blanched almonds or salted peanuts may also be added for a crunchy texture.

To freeze: All meats freeze well, provided they are well wrapped, to retain the natural moisture and flavor of the meat. Always cut the meat into convenient-sized portions, or ask the butcher to do this for you, before wrapping. Bulk buying of meat is a sensible method of saving money, but always check that your family will enjoy all the cuts of meat if you buy half a lamb, etc.

Wrap meat thoroughly in freezer wrap and/or foil and wrap as tightly as possible to exclude the maximum amount of air to hasten freezing and to retard flavor loss. Never try to freeze too much meat at one time; check with your manufacturer's instructions as to the maximum quantity recommended.

When freezing chops, steaks, home-made hamburgers, etc. separate these with squares of foil, then wrap the pile all together or put them into a plastic container. In this way the meat does not stick together but you can "peel off" exactly the number of chops, steaks, etc. you desire.

Use uncooked beef, lamb and mutton within 8–9 months; pork within 6 months; veal within 4 months and salted meats within 3 months.

When the meat is cooked the storage times are roughly halved, but this does depend on the method of cooking and other ingredients added; details are given under the various recipes in this book.

To fry meat: Choose the same cuts as for broiling, page 65. When frying lean meat (e.g. steak) heat a little fat in the pan; fat meat (e.g. bacon and pork) can be fried in its own fat.

Fry quickly on either side to "seal in" the flavor. Time as for broiling, page 65.

Breaded Chops

4 rib lamb chops, 1 inch thick
To coat:
salt and pepper
pinch dried rosemary
1–2 tablespoons flour
1 egg
1 cup soft breadcrumbs
To fry:
¼ cup butter
2 tablespoons oil
To garnish:
8 whole mushrooms
4 small tomatoes
Quick tip:
Use packaged stuffing mix, crushed, instead of making breadcrumbs.

Trim fat from the chops. Mix the salt, pepper and rosemary with the flour, coat the chops in this, then in the beaten egg and crumbs. Heat the butter with the oil in a large frying pan; the oil prevents the butter over-heating and burning. Fry the chops quickly on either side for 2 minutes until golden. Lower the heat for a further 6–8 minutes then add the mushrooms and halved tomatoes sprinkled with salt and pepper and cook for a further 2–4 minutes.
To serve:
As soon as cooked with a green salad.
To vary:
Chops Parmesan: Coat the chops with equal quantities of dry breadcrumbs and grated Parmesan cheese. Fry as above.

Chops in Sweet Sour Sauce: Season the chops with salt and pepper but coat only with the flour. Fry as above, remove from pan and keep hot. Stir ⅔ cup beef broth, 1 tablespoon vinegar and 3 tablespoons redcurrant jelly into any drippings remaining in the pan. Stir over low heat until the jelly has melted then spoon over the meat.
To freeze:
Coat then freeze, or use frozen chops. Use within 6–8 months.
To economize:
Coat with milk and breadcrumbs; omit the egg.

Swiss Steaks

1 onion
2 tablespoons butter or margarine
1½ lbs. ground beef
salt and pepper
pinch fines herbes
1 egg, separated
1–2 tablespoons flour
To fry:
¼ cup fat
Quick tip:
Grate the onion or use instant minced onion.

Grate or chop the peeled onion finely and sauté in the butter or margarine for a few minutes, then mix with the steak, salt, pepper, herbs and egg yolk. Form into 4 thin flat cakes, like a thin minute steak. Brush with the lightly beaten egg white, and coat with flour seasoned with salt and pepper. Fry in the hot fat for 1–2 minutes on either side until firm and golden colored. Lower the heat and continue cooking to personal taste.
To serve:
As fried steak with vegetables and/or salad.
To vary:
These steaks are rather like hamburgers, but the thinner steaks look and taste not unlike ordinary fried minute steaks. The Swiss Steaks can be topped with some of the traditional garnishes for fried steak such as tomato sauce, crumbled blue cheese, slices American cheese.
To freeze:
Prepare, but freeze before cooking. Use within 3 months. Separate each steak with plastic wrap or foil. Cook from the frozen state.
To economize:
Use the cheaper grades of ground beef.

Stuffed Lamb Chops

4 loin lamb chops
2 slices bacon
4 oz. mushrooms
¼ cup butter or fat
1 tablespoon chopped parsley
½ teaspoon chopped mint
¼ cup soft breadcrumbs
salt and pepper
1–2 tablespoons flour

Remove the bones from the chops. These can be simmered in a little water to give stock to serve with the chops. Chop the bacon and mushrooms finely. Heat half the butter or fat and sauté the bacon and mushrooms in this for several minutes. Add the herbs, breadcrumbs and salt and pepper. Press the stuffing together with a spoon and then spread against the side of the chops, where the bones have been removed. Roll as the Noisettes on page 65, tie with fine string or fasten with toothpicks. Dust both sides of the meat with flour mixed with salt and pepper. Heat the remaining butter or fat and fry the stuffed chops until tender; turn very carefully, so the stuffing does not fall out.
To serve:
Hot with salad or cooked vegetables. Stock from bones can be thickened and served as gravy.
To freeze:
Prepare and freeze, ready to cook later. Use within 3 months.
To economize:
This is a good way to use up a few slices bacon and to make a more substantial meal from small chops.

Deep fried steak en croûte

Deep Fried Steak en Croûte

To make: 1 hour **To cook:** 6–7 minutes **Serves 4**

4 "minute" steaks
salt and pepper
2 tablespoons butter
½ cup pâté (see page 24)
puff pastry made with 2 cups
  all-purpose flour, etc. (see page 97)
1 egg
To fry:
deep oil or fat
To garnish:
watercress
Quick tip:
Use purchased liver pâté and frozen
puff pastry which will be very much
quicker.

Season the steaks with salt and pepper and fry for 2–3 minutes in the hot butter, turning once. Lift from the pan, cool then spread with pâté on one side only. Roll out the pastry until only ⅛-inch thickness. Cut into 4 large rounds. Place the meat in the center of each pastry round. Brush the edges with a little beaten egg and seal VERY FIRMLY. Cut any pastry trimmings into leaves for decoration. Brush the outside of each shape with the rest of the egg. Heat the oil, see page 44. Fry for 4 minutes only, drain on absorbent paper and serve at once garnished with watercress.

To vary:
Steak en croûte: This is a classic dish that can be baked, rather than fried. You can choose thicker steaks for baking. Cook to personal taste, prepare as above then bake for 20 minutes in a very hot oven, 475°F., reducing the heat after 10 minutes to 425°F.

To freeze:
Prepare, freeze, but thaw out before cooking. Use within 6 weeks.

To economize:
Use rissoles, see page 94, wrap in pastry and cook as above.

Steak in Pepper Sauce

To make: 8–10 minutes **To cook:** 10–15 minutes **Serves 4**

4 fillet or rump steaks
salt and pepper
6 tablespoons butter
2 canned pimientos
⅔ cup light cream
few drops Tabasco
2 teaspoons chopped parsley

Sprinkle steaks with salt and pepper; be especially generous with the pepper. Heat the butter in a large frying pan and cook the steaks on either side to taste. Lift out of the pan and keep warm. Add the diced pimientos, cream, Tabasco sauce and parsley to the meat juices remaining in the pan. Stir over low heat for 2–3 minutes, then spoon over the steaks.

To freeze:
Do not freeze this dish, but frozen steaks could be used.

Piquant veal scalloppini

Piquant Veal Scalloppini

To make: 10 minutes   **To cook:** 15 minutes   **Serves 4**

4 slices veal scalloppini
salt and pepper
3 tablespoons flour
¼ cup butter, see method
6 green onions
1 lemon
1–2 teaspoons chopped rosemary
¼ teaspoon Tabasco
⅔ cup dry vermouth
To garnish:
1 tablespoon chopped parsley
Quick tip:
Simply season veal, do not coat with flour.

Pound the meat until very thin, then cut each scalloppini in half. Sprinkle with salt and pepper. Coat with flour. Heat the butter and fry veal until golden, turning once. Remove from the pan and keep hot. Chop the green onions, but keep the white and green parts separate. Add a little more butter to the pan if necessary and fry the white part of the onions until soft. Replace the veal, add the thinly sliced unpeeled lemon, rosemary, Tabasco and vermouth. Simmer for 2–3 minutes. Season with salt and pepper and sprinkle with the chopped green part of the onions and chopped parsley.
To serve:
With mixed vegetables.
To vary:
Use sour cream in place of vermouth, or hard cider.
   Add chopped white fennel and a small amount of chopped fennel leaves to the mixture.
   Scalloppini Turin-style: Coat the slices of veal with salt, pepper and flour. Dip into beaten egg and then a mixture of dry breadcrumbs and grated Parmesan cheese. Fry in hot butter as the recipe above. Top with tomato slices and anchovy fillets and serve with lemon and a green salad (illustrated opposite).
To freeze:
Do not freeze this dish, but frozen veal could be used.
To economize:
Use thin slices pork, if cheaper than veal; hard cider instead of vermouth.

Sweet & Sour Pork

To make: 15 minutes   **To cook:** 25 minutes   **Serves 4–6**

1½ lbs. pork tenderloin (cut from the leg)
3 tablespoons cornstarch
salt and pepper
little oil or fat for frying
3 canned pineapple rings
⅓ cup pineapple syrup
4 tablespoons cocktail onions
3 tablespoons vinegar
1¼ cups stock or water and 1 chicken bouillon cube
1 tablespoon honey
3 tablespoons sherry
2 teaspoons soy sauce
1 tablespoon tomato ketchup

Cut the meat into 1-inch cubes. Dust with half the cornstarch, blended with a little salt and pepper and fry slowly in the hot oil or fat until tender. Place on serving dish and keep hot. Meanwhile hop the pineapple slices and put into a saucepan with the pineapple syrup, onions, vinegar, stock or water and bouillon cube, blended with the remaining cornstarch and the rest of the ingredients. Stir over low heat until thickened and smooth. Spoon over the pork.
To serve:
As soon as cooked, so the pork does not become too tough in the sauce. A green salad is a good accompaniment, or bamboo shoots, or bean sprouts and cooked rice.
To vary:
Use diced steak or other meat, or diced chicken.
To freeze:
This dish does not freeze, but frozen meat could be used.

Fried Bacon & Egg

To make: 5 minutes **To cook:** 4–7 minutes **Serves 4**

8 slices Canadian bacon
little extra fat if the bacon is very lean
4 eggs

Fry bacon until lightly browned on both sides. Keep warm. Push bacon to one side, fry eggs until whites are firm and yolks are soft, with extra fat if needed.

Veal Chops with Tomato Sauce

To make: 15 minutes **To cook:** 20–25 minutes **Serves 4**

4 veal chops
salt and pepper
¼ cup butter
1 slice bacon
1 onion
1 can (16 oz.) plum tomatoes
1 teaspoon cornstarch
⅓ cup broth or water

Season the veal with salt and pepper, fry in the hot butter until tender; veal, like pork, must be well cooked. Remove from the pan and keep hot. Chop the bacon and onion. Fry in any fat remaining in the pan for 2–3 minutes; do not allow the onion to brown or the bacon to become crisp. Add the tomatoes, then the cornstarch blended with the broth or water. Bring to a boil, lower the heat and stir until thickened. If the sauce is rather thick, add extra liquid. Serve sauce over the chops.
To freeze:
Do not freeze this dish, but frozen veal could be used, see page 56.

Adding Flavors

Bacon and apple: Apple rings are delicious with fried bacon. Fry bacon slices until crisp. Put in thin slices cored cooking apples (peel if desired), cook for 2–3 minutes, turning once.

Bacon and cheese: Fry or broil bacon slices, add thick slices Cheddar or Gruyère cheese towards end of the cooking time.

Curried chops: Season pork, veal or lamb chops with salt and pepper and add a sprinkling of curry powder. Fry or broil in the usual way.

Paprika chops: Season pork or veal chops with salt and pepper then fry in the usual way. Lift out of the pan and keep hot. Blend 1–2 teaspoons paprika and 1–2 teaspoons chopped chives with ⅔ cup white wine. Pour into the pan and stir to absorb all the meat juices, heat thoroughly. Beat in ¼ cup heavy cream, heat without boiling then spoon over the chops.

Steak Diane: Heat a generous amount of butter in a pan, fry 1–2 thinly sliced or chopped onions and thin slices sirloin steak sprinkled with salt and pepper, until tender. Add 1 teaspoon Worcestershire sauce, 1 tablespoon brandy and 1 tablespoon chopped parsley. Heat for 1 minute and serve. Veal or pork fillets can be cooked in the same way.

Scalloppini Turin-style

Sausage Patties

These are a great favorite with children. Buy bulk sausage or remove skin from sausages and mix with a few raisins, some finely chopped peeled apple and a few chopped nuts. Form into flat cakes, brush with egg and roll in crumbs or crushed potato chips. Fry slowly in 2 tablespoons shortening until well done.

Pork with Spicy Orange Sauce

To make: 15 minutes   **To cook:** 30 minutes   **Serves 4**

1½ lbs. pork tenderloin (cut from the leg)
¼ cup flour
salt and pepper
3 navel oranges
1 small onion
1 green pepper
2 tablespoons butter
1 tablespoon Worcestershire sauce
⅔ cup beef stock or water and 1 beef bouillon cube

Quick tip:
Use instant minced onion, canned orange juice and canned mandarin oranges.

Trim the pork and cut into 1-inch cubes. Coat with flour mixed with salt and pepper. Grate the rind from one orange, then cut away peel and cut into sections. Squeeze out juice from the remaining two oranges. Chop the onion and pepper (discard seeds) and fry in the hot butter for 3 minutes. Add the pork and cook for 5 minutes, turning frequently. Stir in the orange juice, grated orange rind, Worcestershire sauce and stock, or water and bouillon cube. Bring to a boil and simmer for 20 minutes, stirring occasionally. Season to taste and add the orange sections just before serving.

To serve:
A green salad and cooked rice are good accompaniments.

To vary:
Use duck in place of pork; remove skin before dicing.

To freeze:
Do not freeze this dish if you want to retain the slightly firm texture of the onion and pepper, otherwise freeze and use within 3 months.

To economize:
Use cheaper cuts of pork. Simmer for 15 minutes in broth, drain, coat in seasoned flour and proceed as recipe.

Pork with spicy orange sauce

Pork with Barbecue Sauce

To make: 15 minutes   **To cook:** 1 hour and 20 minutes   **Serves 4–6**

3 lbs. country-style pork ribs
2 tablespoons oil
1 cup beef broth
2 medium-sized onions
3 tablespoons tomato paste
3 tablespoons water
3 tablespoons firmly packed brown
   sugar
3 tablespoons vinegar
1 teaspoon Worcestershire sauce
1–2 teaspoons prepared mustard
pinch fines herbes
salt and pepper
Quick tip:
Use instant minced onion.

Cut ribs into individual ribs. Heat the oil in a pan and fry the ribs slowly on both sides until lightly browned. Drain excess fat. Add broth, cover and simmer for 1 hour or until tender. Remove ribs from the pan and put on a plate. Add the chopped onions to the pan, simmer for 5 minutes, then stir in the remaining ingredients and bring to a boil. Replace the ribs in the pan, cover and simmer for 15 minutes.

To serve:
With a green salad.
To vary:
Use lamb chops, without the broth.
To freeze:
Do not freeze this dish although frozen pork can be cooked from the frozen state.
To economize:
Use hip pork chops instead of ribs.

Pork Normandy

To make: 10 minutes   **To cook:** 20–25 minutes   **Serves 4**

4 pork chops
2 medium-sized onions
2 medium-sized apples
2 tablespoons butter
pinch dried sage
salt and pepper
⅔ cup light cream
¼–⅓ cup Calvados

Fry the pork chops slowly until tender. Lift out of the pan and keep hot. Drain excess fat. Finely chop the onion and peel, core and thinly slice the apples. Heat the butter in the pan used for cooking chops and fry the onions with the sage, salt and pepper and apples for 5 minutes. Add the cream and Calvados and heat, without boiling. Stir well to absorb the meat juices and pour over the chops and serve with green salad.

To freeze:
This dish does not freeze well, but you can use frozen pork chops.

Pork with barbecue sauce

Meats for Broiling

The meat you broil must be tender and of prime quality, as broiling is a quick method of cooking. Always pre-heat the broiler except when cooking bacon, see page 66.

When broiling beef:
Choose thin (minute) steaks, shell, rump, porterhouse, T-bone, fillet mignon or sirloin, flank steak.

When broiling pork or veal:
Choose loin or rib chops, cutlets or thin slices (fillets) from the leg.

When broiling lamb:
Choose loin or rib lamb chops or cutlets or thin slices (fillets) from the leg.
   Keep lean meat well basted with melted butter or oil during cooking; unless marinated as kebabs, page 66.
   Do not over-cook the meat and do not keep it waiting before serving, otherwise it could become dry and less appetizing.
   Cook the meat quickly at the beginning; this "seals-in" the meat juices. You can then lower the heat of the broiler and/or lower the position of the broiler pan so the meat cooks more slowly; this means it is cooked through to the center without over-cooking the outside.

Time for broiling and frying meats:
Cook chops or cutlets quickly for 1–2 minutes on either side. Lower the heat, continue cooking for about 8 minutes, or a little longer for pork and veal. Time for steaks varies with personal taste. Seal the outside quickly, (thin "minute" steaks would then be ready). For ½–¾ inch "rare" steaks, lower the heat and cook for a further 2–3 minutes; for medium to well cooked steaks, cook for a further 4–8 minutes.

Noisettes of lamb

Noisettes of Lamb

To make: 15 minutes   **To cook:** 10–12 minutes   **Serves 4**

8 rib or loin of lamb chops
salt and pepper
pinch dried rosemary
Maître d'hôtel butter:
¼ cup butter
½–1 tablespoon chopped parsley
few drops lemon juice
salt and pepper

First make the Maître d'hôtel butter. Cream the butter with the parsley, lemon juice and seasoning. Form into a 1 inch in diameter roll, chill until hard and cut into rounds before serving. Remove the bones from the chops, tie the meat into rounds with string. Sprinkle with salt and pepper and the rosemary. Broil as above; there is no need to brush with additional fat as the natural fat from the meat is sufficient. Top with the butter just before serving.

To serve:
On rounds of fried bread or toast with mixed vegetables and salad.

To freeze:
Prepare noisettes, freeze. Use within 6–8 months. Cook from the frozen state.

Broiled lamb chops

Broiled Ham Steaks

To make: 5 minutes **To cook:** 10–12 minutes **Serves 4**

4 smoked ham steaks, boneless and
   tenderized
¼ cup butter (see method)
tomatoes, mushrooms, fruit (see
   method)
salt and pepper and/or sugar

Brush ham with melted butter. Broil quickly for 5–6 minutes, turn, brush with more butter and cook on the second side 5–6 minutes. Tomatoes and mushrooms can be cooked with the ham. Either broil on broiler pan with salt, pepper and butter, or add to the rack towards the end of the cooking time.

   Fruits — peaches, pineapple, pears, orange slices, apple rings, etc. all blend well with ham. Brush the fruit with butter so it does not dry, and broil for a few minutes. To give an attractive glaze sprinkle the fruit and the edge of the ham with very little brown sugar.

Note:
Snip the fat at the edge of the ham at regular intervals with kitchen scissors before cooking to prevent curling.

To serve:
Hot with creamed or fried potatoes, green vegetables or salad.

To freeze:
Do not freeze broiled ham, but you can use frozen ham.

Roast pork

Sausages & Bacon with Mustard Sauce

To make: 10 minutes **To cook:** 15–20 minutes **Serves 4**

1 tablespoon fat
1 lb. pork or beef sausages
8 slices bacon
For the sauce:
2 tablespoons margarine (see method)
¼ cup flour
½–1 tablespoon dry mustard
⅔ cup milk
⅔ cup stock or water and ½ beef
   bouillon cube
salt and pepper

Heat fat in frying pan. Fry the sausages and then the bacon until ready to serve. Put on a hot dish while making the sauce in the frying pan; this is not only quicker, but gives the sauce more flavor. If you have plenty of fat left in the pan, there is no need to use the amount of margarine given. Stir the flour and mustard into the fat, then stir in the milk and stock or water and bouillon cube. Bring slowly to a boil and cook, stirring well, until smooth and thickened, season to taste with salt and pepper.

To serve:
Pour the sauce carefully over the sausages, but not the bacon. Serve at once with creamed potatoes and peas or beans.

Herbed Kebabs

To make: 10 minutes plus marinating **To cook:** 20 minutes **Serves 4**

1 lb. tender lean meat, lamb, pork or
   beef, or use a mixture of meats
12 button mushrooms
1 green pepper
⅔ cup long grain rice
1¼ cups water
salt and pepper
For the marinade:
3 tablespoons oil
⅓ cup wine vinegar
salt and pepper
1 tablespoon chopped mixed fresh
   herbs

Cut meat into 1-inch cubes and put into the marinade, made by mixing the oil, vinegar, salt, pepper and herbs; adapt the herbs according to the meats used, i.e., if choosing mainly pork, add plenty of sage, rosemary with lamb, chives and crushed garlic with beef. Leave for 1–2 hours. Wash, but do not peel the mushrooms, cut the pepper into 1-inch squares (discard seeds). Lift the meat from the marinade and spear on 4 long metal skewers alternating with the mushrooms and green pepper. Put the rice with the cold water and salt to taste into a saucepan. Bring the water to a boil, stir with a fork, lower the heat and cover the pan. Simmer gently for 15 minutes, by which time the rice should be cooked and the liquid absorbed. Broil the kebabs, turning once or twice and basting with any left-over marinade.

To serve:
Hot on the bed of hot rice and with a mixed or green salad.

To vary:
Use small par-boiled onions and tomatoes with the meat.

To freeze:
Dice then freeze meats for kebabs or freeze sausages. Diced meat should be stored for half the time given on page 56 for roasts.

To economize:
Use sausages or meat balls, see page 78, in place of the diced meat; marinate sausages, but not meat balls.

To Roast Meat

Roasting is a simple method of cooking and can be done in the oven or under a rotisserie; the time for roasting in this manner is the same as for quick roasting, see page 87 and under "Timing" for the individual meats.

Select the meat you roast most carefully, it must be of prime quality and the right cuts for successful cooking.

It is possible to roast meat in the same three ways as poultry, on page 87, although the ultra slow method is rarely used.

Frozen meat:

If roasting frozen roasts either allow them to defrost thoroughly, this will take about 24 hours for a 4–5 lb. roast at room temperature, or almost twice as long in the refrigerator, or cook from the frozen state. If you use this method then do not attempt to roast by the quick method but the slower way (this does not mean the ultra slow method). Allow 50% longer cooking time than when roasting a fresh or defrosted roast, or use a meat thermometer, which will indicate the degree of cooking for you. Opinions vary as to which method is better, a) defrosting the meat first or b) cooking more slowly. Personally, I am inclined to think the latter is more satisfactory as you seem to retain more of the natural meat juices. However, try both methods and decide for yourself.

To roast pork:

One important rule when you cook pork by any method is to make absolutely certain the meat is thoroughly cooked. Under-cooked pork can cause food poisoning and trichinosis.

To give a crisp crackling to the skin of pork, score and rub with olive oil or melted lard. You can sprinkle it lightly with salt, but this is not essential. Use an open roasting pan.

Roasts to choose:

Beef — fillet, rib, sirloin, eye round, bottom round, rolled rib roasts. Lamb — rack, leg. Pork — fresh ham, loin, shoulder, smoked ham.

Timing:

If using the quick roasting method on page 87 allow 25 minutes per pound and 25 minutes over. If using the slower roasting method then 35 minutes per pound and 35 minutes additional. For the ultra slow roasting allow 2½ hours for the first lb., then follow timing as for chicken. Serve with sage and onion stuffing and apple sauce or the cherry or orange sauces given for duckling on page 89, or a thickened gravy.

A new look to pork:

Roast peeled onions, sprinkled with salt and pepper and sage, and whole peeled apples, rolled in the pork fat and sprinkled with a little sugar, around the pork roast as shown in the picture.

67

To Roast Beef

Roast beef is one of the most delicious roasts. When buying the beef see there is a good "marbling" of fat, as this makes sure it will be moist when cooked. If you add fat to beef use very little, as too much will harden the surface of the meat. You can use an open roasting pan or cover with foil, put into a plastic cooking bag or into a covered pan. If using either of these last three methods allow about 15–20 minutes extra cooking time, see page 87 for details of this.

Roasts to choose:
Fillet, rib, rump, sirloin, rolled rib, eye round, bottom round.

Timing:
If using the quick roasting method, see page 87, allow 15 minutes per pound and 15 minutes additional for rare meat, 20 minutes per pound and 20 minutes additional for medium to well-done. If using the slower method then allow 25 minutes per pound and 25 minutes additional. For well-done beef add 15–20 minutes to the total time.

If you would like to follow the ultra slow method then allow just the same time as for chicken if you like your beef medium-rare.

Serve beef with mustard and horseradish cream or sauce, see page 82, Yorkshire pudding, below, and pan juices.

Yorkshire Pudding

One of the essentials of a good Yorkshire pudding is to cook it quickly so you must choose the quick method of roasting on this occasion. In fact I prefer to raise the oven temperature by 25°F. to 425°F. when I put the pudding into the oven; leave it at this high temperature for 10–15 minutes, then lower the heat for the rest of the cooking time to 400°F.

To make the batter:
Sift 1 cup all-purpose flour and a pinch of salt. Gradually beat in 1 large egg and 1¼ cups milk. Stand in a cool place until ready to bake.

If you prefer to cook the pudding under the meat, remove the roasting pan from the oven and pour out all the fat except for 1 tablespoon. Heat this again on top of range; then pour in the batter. Put the beef on a high trivet over the pudding and bake; the flavor is magnificent, but the pudding does not rise as when cooked by the more usual method below. To give a very well risen pudding heat about 3 tablespoons (no more) fat or drippings in a 9-inch square baking pan, pour in the batter and bake in a very hot oven, 450°F., reducing the heat to 400°F. after 10–15 minutes. Bake another 30 minutes until well-risen and brown. Individual puddings baked in custard cups take about 15 minutes at 400°F.

Stuffed Fillet of Beef

To make: 15 minutes   **To cook:** 1¼–1½ hours   **Serves 4**

1 lb. fillet of beef, in one piece
2 onions
¼ cup drippings (see method)
2 anchovy fillets
1 tablespoon chopped bacon
pinch of pepper
pinch of dried thyme
½ teaspoon finely chopped parsley
1 egg yolk
To garnish:
watercress
Quick tip:
Use a little bulk sausage flavored with chopped anchovy fillets for the stuffing.

Remove excess fat from beef. Chop or slice the onions. Sauté the onions in 2 tablespoons of the drippings until they are golden brown. Remove from the pan and place in a mixing bowl. Stir in the chopped anchovy fillets, bacon, pepper, thyme, parsley and the beaten egg yolk. Cut the fillet lengthwise in about 4 places, but not right through. Put some of the stuffing into each cut and tie the fillet up with string or fasten with toothpicks. Either wrap in greased foil, put into a plastic cooking bag or place in a roasting pan with the remaining drippings and cook in a low oven, 300°F. for 1–1¼ hours, or until tender.

To serve:
Hot, cut into thick slices, with cooked vegetables and garnished with watercress.

To vary:
Use any other stuffing, see pages 82 and 83.

To freeze:
Prepare the fillet, wrap and freeze. Thaw out before cooking. Use within 4–5 months.

To economize:
Use a piece of eye round, about 2 lbs., instead of fillet. As this is inclined to dry slightly, baste with a little broth during cooking, unless cooking in a bag, and allow 1½–1¾ hours in the slow oven.

Stuffed fillet of beef

To Roast Lamb

Lamb should always be tender when roasted, provided you choose the correct roast, but take care to roast only tender young lamb. There should be no need to add extra fat with lamb. You can use an open roasting pan or cover with foil, put into a plastic cooking bag or into a covered pan. If using either of these last three methods allow about 15–20 minutes extra cooking time, see page 87 for details of this.

Roasts to choose:
Lamb neck, breast (this is an economical but rather fatty roast that can be boned, covered with a stuffing then rolled), leg, loin, saddle (this is a double loin and ideal for parties), shoulder. Another very impressive roast of lamb is a Crown Roast. This consists of 2 racks of lamb loin chops shaped into a "crown". The center can be filled with a favorite stuffing.

Timing:
Allow 20 minutes per pound and 20 minutes additional if using the quick roasting method on page 87. If you like very young lamb slightly "pink" as in France, then reduce the total cooking time by about 15 minutes. If you prefer the slower roasting time then give 35 minutes per pound and 35 minutes additional. Serve lamb with mint sauce, page 82.

To Roast Veal

Veal is an exceptionally lean meat and must be kept well basted with fat during cooking. It also needs adequate cooking. Either "lard" the veal or cover with plenty of fat bacon or fat. To "lard" veal, cut very thin strips of fat pork or bacon and thread through the raw meat with a "larding" needle.

Roasts to choose:
Breast, fillet, leg loin or loin shoulder.

Timing:
This is exactly the same as for pork on page 67.

To serve:
Serve veal with bacon, sausages and bread sauce, see page 88, with veal stuffing, page 83, and thickened gravy.

A new look to veal:
Although cranberry sauce is not a usual accompaniment to veal I find it blends very well indeed. I often flavor the gravy with port wine.

To Make Interesting Stews

A stew can be one of the most delicious, as well as economical dishes and basic methods of stewing are given in the recipes opposite. As you will see some stews do not have a thickened liquid, but in others the meat is first browned to seal in the flavor, then cooked in a thickened sauce.

It is easy to change the flavor of a stew; simply use different vegetables, more herbs, add various spices or Worcestershire sauce or soy sauce. Put in a pinch of curry powder and a few drops of Tabasco or use some wine in the liquid, see also page 76.

Casseroles

Most stews can be cooked in a covered dish in a slow oven, 325°F. rather than in a covered saucepan. If you adapt the recipe to cook in the oven, reduce the amount of liquid by 25% as there is less evaporation in the oven than on top of the range.

Pork and bamboo shoots

Pork & Bamboo Shoots

To make: 15 minutes　**To cook:** 1 hour 20 minutes　**Serves 6–8**

2 lbs. lean boneless pork
3–4 tablespoons soy sauce
1½–2 tablespoons sherry
1 teaspoon brown sugar
1 teaspoon ground ginger
salt and pepper
5 cups water
1 can (5 oz.) bamboo shoots
1 tablespoon cornstarch
Quick tip:
Use diced tenderloin of pork, mix with the soy sauce, etc., then fry in hot oil until tender. Heat the bamboo shoots separately and serve around the pork.

Cut the pork into small ¾-inch cubes. Mix the soy sauce, sherry, sugar, ginger and salt and pepper together. Add to the pork, toss well and leave for 10 minutes. Put the pork and flavorings into a large pan, add 3½ cups of the water and bring gently to a boil, cover and simmer for 1 hour. Wash and drain bamboo shoots and shred finely. Add to the pan and simmer for another 10 minutes. Mix the cornstarch with the remaining water, stir into the pan and continue cooking for 10 minutes, stirring from time to time until thickened.

To serve:
With extra soy sauce.
To vary:
Use diced raw chicken or other meat instead of pork.
To freeze:
This dish is better not frozen.
To economize:
Use shoulder or boned hip chops.

Goulash

To make: 20 minutes **To cook:** 2 hours and 15 minutes **Serves 4–6**

1 lb. boneless beef chuck or round
8 oz. boneless veal
¼ cup drippings or butter
2–3 medium-sized onions
1 clove garlic (optional)
1 lb. tomatoes
salt and pepper
½–1 tablespoon sweet paprika
2½ cups stock or water and 2 beef
    bouillon cubes
1 lb. peeled potatoes
To garnish:
chopped parsley
1 cup plain yogurt
Quick tip:
See Savory Beef Stew (below).

Cut meats into 1-inch cubes then brown for a few minutes in the hot drippings or butter in a good-sized saucepan. Remove the meat, add the sliced onions, chopped garlic and sauté for 2–3 minutes. Return the meat to the pan with the skinned diced tomatoes, salt, pepper and paprika, mixed with the stock or water and bouillon cube. Cover the pan and simmer gently for 1¾ hours. Thickly slice the potatoes if large or leave whole if small. Add to the pan, cover and continue cooking gently for nearly 30 minutes or until potatoes are tender.
To serve:
Spoon on a hot dish and top with parsley and yogurt.
To vary:
Omit the potatoes in the stew and use a little less liquid; serve with noodles.
Add 1–2 teaspoons caraway seeds.
Use all beef, veal, or a mixture of veal and pork.
To freeze:
This freezes well, use within 2 months for the best flavor.

Savory Beef Stew

To make: 20 minutes **To cook:** 2½ hours **Serves 4–6**

1½ lbs. boneless beef chuck
salt and pepper
¼ cup flour
¼ cup drippings or fat
3–4 large onions
2½ cups stock or water and 2 beef
    bouillon cubes
4–5 large carrots
2 small yellow turnips
bouquet garni (see page 28)
Quick tip:
Use a pressure cooker for the Goulash and this stew. For beef stew, allow 15 minutes at 15 lb. pressure. For Goulash, reduce the pressure after 10 minutes, add potatoes then cook at the same pressure for an additional 5 minutes.

Cut the meat into 1-inch cubes. Mix the salt and pepper and flour, then coat the meat. Brown in the hot drippings or fat for several minutes, remove from the pan. Add the sliced onions and sauté these gently until transparent. Gradually mix in the stock or water and bouillon cubes and stir over low heat until a thin sauce. Add the meat, sliced or diced carrots and turnips, together with the herbs tied in muslin or with cotton. Cover the pan and simmer gently until the meat is tender, about 1½ hours. Season to taste with salt and pepper.
To serve:
With dumplings, see page 75, creamed or boiled potatoes and a green vegetable. Remove bouquet garni before serving.
To vary:
Use other vegetables and flavorings, see opposite and page 76. Cook in a covered casserole in a slow oven, 300°F. for the same length of time.
To freeze:
This dish, like most stews, freezes well; use within 3 months.
To economize:
Use less meat and add protein vegetables — peas, beans, etc.

Spring Lamb

To make: 25 minutes **To cook:** 1½ hours **Serves 4–6**

3 lbs. neck of lamb
salt and pepper
12 small white onions
1 lb. young carrots
1 lb. lima beans (fresh)
1 lb. new potatoes
small bunch mint
To garnish:
cucumber sauce (see method)
Quick tip:
Use a pressure cooker, cook for 12 minutes at 15 lb. pressure.

Cover lamb with water in a pan and add salt and pepper. Bring the water to a boil, skim any "scum" from the surface, then add the peeled onions and sliced carrots. Cover the pan and simmer gently for almost 1 hour. Meanwhile shell the beans and peel the potatoes; add to the lamb together with the mint, tied with string, and salt and pepper to taste. Simmer gently for another 30 minutes.
To serve:
Lift the meat and vegetables from the broth with a slotted spoon on a hot dish. Top with the hot cucumber sauce, see below.
To vary:
Use vegetables in season, serve with a caper sauce. This is made by adding 2–3 teaspoons capers, plus a little vinegar from the bottle, instead of cucumber in the sauce below.
Cucumber sauce:
Make a white sauce, as page 54, but using half milk and half lamb stock. When thickened add half a diced peeled cucumber, plus 1–2 teaspoons cider vinegar; heat gently, but do not boil.
To freeze:
Undercook slightly; use within 2 months.
To economize:
Do not waste the stock, use in Mulligatawny soup, see page 36.

Meat Pies & Puddings

A really light meat pudding is one of the most satisfying cold weather dishes. I have given the best known of all meat puddings on this page, but other meats and flavorings can be used, as you will see from the suggested variations.

When you make a meat pie you have a wide choice of pastries. There is the very light puff pastry, commercially frozen, as page 73, or home-made, page 97. The best known and easiest pastry to make, i.e., pie crust, is given on page 122.

In the lamb pie below, the pastry is a hot water crust, typical of English meat pies.

English Steak & Kidney Pudding

2 cups self-rising or all-purpose flour
  (see note under method)
pinch salt
½ cup finely chopped or ground suet
water to mix
For the filling:
1 lb. good quality chuck or flank steak
8 oz. beef kidney
1 tablespoon flour
salt and pepper
3–4 tablespoons stock or water

To make: 25–30 minutes   **To cook:** 4–5 hours   **Serves 4–6**

Sift the flour, or flour and baking powder (see Note), and salt. Stir in suet. Stir in enough water to make a stiff dough. Roll out thinly as this pastry rises. Line a 1 quart pudding basin or heatproof bowl with nearly three-quarters of the dough, leaving a good quarter for the lid. Dice the meat and kidney into ½ inch cubes and roll in the flour mixed with the salt and pepper. Put into the lined bowl and add the stock or water. Roll out the remaining dough to a round large enough to cover top. Press over the filling. Seal at the edges. Cover with greased waxed paper and foil. Place bowl in a large kettle with boiling water ¾ up the sides. Steam or boil rapidly for 4–5 hours. For a good result make sure that the water is boiling rapidly when the pudding starts to cook and keep up the level of the liquid with the addition of more boiling water.

Note:
If you like a light, well risen crust use self-rising flour or all-purpose flour with 1–2 teaspoons baking powder. If you prefer a thin, unrisen crust, use all-purpose flour. For a thicker crust use 2½ cups all-purpose flour, etc.

To vary:
Bacon and vegetable pudding: use diced thick bacon slices, a mixture of vegetables and tomato juice instead of the stock or water.

Chicken pudding: use diced raw chicken and vegetables; flavor with a pinch of mixed herbs or add tiny balls of veal stuffing, see page 83.

Lamb pudding: use diced lamb and lambs' kidneys in place of steak and kidney.

To economize:
Use less meat and add onions and other vegetables.

Old-fashioned Lamb Pie

To make: 35 minutes   **To cook:** 2¾ hours   **Serves 5–6**

2 lbs. boneless lamb, cut from the leg
salt and pepper
bouquet garni (see method)
1–2 onions
3 eggs
For the hot water crust pastry:
3 cups all-purpose flour
pinch salt
⅔ cup lard
⅔ cup water
To glaze:
1 egg
Quick tip:
Make individual pies and bake for 1¼ hours.

Cut the meat into small 1-inch cubes, put into a pan with very little water, salt and pepper and the bouquet garni. (Use just one tiny sprig of mint as well as parsley, sage, chives.) Simmer gently in the covered pan for only 30 minutes. Meanwhile chop the onions finely, hard-cook and shell the eggs and make the pastry. Sift the flour and salt, heat the lard and water until the lard has melted. Pour the hot lard mixture on the flour, stir and then knead until smooth. Roll out to ¼-inch thickness and cut a strip for the sides of a 7-inch cake pan 2 inches deep and two 7-inch rounds for the top and bottom of the pan. Keep the pastry warm. Put one round into the lightly greased pan, moisten the edges with water, then put in the strip of pastry and seal firmly. Drain the meat, pack half into the pan with half the onions and a little salt and pepper. Add the eggs, then the rest of the meat, onions and salt and pepper, press down firmly. Add 2 tablespoons only of the stock. Cover with the remaining round of pastry, sealing the edges firmly. Make a 1-inch hole in the top of the pastry for the steam to escape. Cut leaves and make a rose shape from the left-over pastry, moisten and press on the top, but not over the center hole. Brush the pastry with beaten egg. Bake for 2¼ hours in moderate oven, 350°F. lowering the heat to 325°F. after 1¼ hours. Cool in the pan.

To serve:
Serve this pie when freshly made, do not store.

To economize:
Use half lamb and half bulk sausage.

Steak and kidney pie

Steak & Kidney Pie

To make: 25–30 minutes   **To cook:** 3 hours   **Serves 4–6**

¼ cup lard or drippings
1 large onion
1½ lb. mixed round steak and kidney
¼ cup flour
2 cups water
salt and pepper
1 lb. frozen puff pastry
To glaze:
egg or milk
Quick tip:
Use canned beef stew.

Heat the lard or drippings in a pan, add chopped onion and sauté for 5 minutes. Add the steak and kidney cut into 1 inch cubes and cook gently, stirring, for 5 minutes. Stir in the flour, lower the heat and cook, stirring two or three times for a further 10 minutes. Gradually stir in the water and add salt and pepper. Cover the pan and simmer gently, stirring from time to time, for about 1½–2 hours or until the meat is tender. Remove the pan from the heat and allow the meat to cool. When cold, pour the meat and gravy into a 9-inch pie pan. Roll out the pastry to an oval, just a little bigger than the 9-inch pie pan. Roll puff pastry to ½-inch thickness and cut a strip ½-inch wide. Moisten the rim of the pie pan with water and place this strip all the way around. Moisten the pastry strip with water and carefully place the remaining rolled-out pastry over the top of the pie dish. Trim off the edges of the pastry with a sharp knife. Flute edges. Roll out the pastry trimmings and cut out diamond shapes for leaves. Moisten the leaves with water and arrange in the center of the pie. Brush with a little egg or milk before baking to give it a golden shine. Bake the pie in a very hot oven, 450°F. for 10 minutes, then lower the heat 375–400°F. for a further 15–20 minutes.
To serve:
Hot with vegetables.
To vary:
Use other stewing meat with vegetables to flavor. Make pie crust or puff pastry with 2 cups all-purpose flour, see page 72.
To freeze:
Put the meat into the pie dish and top with the pastry. Freeze, cover and use within 3–4 months. Thaw out before cooking. If preferred, cook then freeze and reheat gently.
To economize:
Use a smaller quantity of meat with diced mixed vegetables.

Glazed ham with apricots

To Boil Meat

The terms "boiled ham", "boiled beef", etc. are widely used, but care must be taken that the liquid in which the meat is cooked does not boil, but just simmers gently.

While all meats can be simmered in the same way as the recipes that follow, this method is most suitable for salted meats, i.e. ham, tongue, brisket, etc.

In order to keep the meat moist, allow it to cool in the liquid in the pan. If you plan to serve some of the meat as a hot dish, carve the required amount for the hot meal, then return the meat to the liquid. The purpose of cooling the meat in this way is to prevent the outside hardening and to keep the meat very moist.

Make quite sure salted meats are covered with liquid when cooking, and read the comments about soaking in the recipes. When storing salted meats wrap well, as they have a tendency to harden.

To Freeze Meat

Wrap well when cold. It is a good idea to slice some of the meat, separating each slice with plastic wrap or foil, so you may "peel off" slices as required. Salted meats do not store as well as fresh meats, so store uncooked salted meats for 3 months and cooked salted meats for 1 month.

Do not waste the stock from boiled meats; this is excellent in soups.

Glazed Ham

The picture above is of glazed ham. This is a delicious way to serve a ham.

While you can roast a milk cure ham in just the same way as pork, and for the same time, see page 67, it is better to par-boil the meat first and then to roast for a short time only. Omit par-boiling if ham is tenderized.

Weigh the ham first and boil for the time required, LESS 30 minutes, see opposite. When the ham is ready to come out of the liquid, drain it well, score (cut) the fat and stud with whole cloves, if wished. Cover the fat with the selected glaze. Roast for 30 minutes in a moderately hot oven, 375–400°F. Check that the glaze, which is generally fairly sweet, is not becoming too brown — if so, lower the heat slightly.

Simple Glazes for Ham

Apricot and ginger:
Mix brown sugar with a little apricot syrup (from canned or cooked apricots) and ground ginger to taste. Add the apricots to the pan for the last 5 minutes cooking.

Honey glaze:
Mix honey with cinnamon, nutmeg and ginger to taste, spread over fat.

Orange glaze:
Mix the finely grated rind and juice of 2 oranges, ½–1 tablespoon prepared mustard and ¾ cup firmly packed brown sugar. Spread over the fat. Serve with orange slices.

Wine and cherry glaze:
Mix ⅔ cup red wine, the syrup from a medium-sized can of dark sweet cherries, 3 tablespoons of soy sauce and 1 teaspoon vinegar. Spoon some over the ham. Baste once or twice during cooking. Add the cherries to the pan for the last few minutes cooking. Serve remaining basting liquid heated as a sauce.

Boiled Ham & Vegetables

To make: 25 minutes plus soaking   **To cook:** see method   **Serves: See below**

smoked ham*
pepper or peppercorns
mixed vegetables, e.g. carrots,
    cabbage, onions, turnips
*allow 6–8 oz. uncooked meat per
person
Quick tip:
Simmer slices of back or Canadian
bacon or ham for 10–15 minutes only.

If buying cured ham soak in cold water to cover. If you like a very mild flavor soak overnight, otherwise for several hours. Canadian bacon and "sweet-cure" hams do not require soaking. Some hams can be cooked in their plastic wrapping, piercing a hole if directed to do so. Put the ham in fresh cold water to cover, add pepper or peppercorns and mixed vegetables. Bring the liquid to the boiling point only, remove any grey bubbles if they form on the surface. Lower the heat and simmer gently for 20 minutes per pound and 20 minutes additional for ham, but up to 35 minutes per pound and 35 minutes additional for the less tender ham hock or shoulder.

To serve:
Hot with the vegetables and parsley sauce, see page 82; use some of the ham stock in the sauce instead of all milk. Cold with salad. Cool the ham, or part of the ham (see opposite page) in the stock. Remove, drain and cut away the skin. Coat the fat with fine crisp breadcrumbs or brown sugar.

To vary:
Add dumplings toward the end of the cooking time, below. Use cider, wine or ginger ale instead of all or some of the water.

To economize:
Choose the cheaper ham hock or shoulder.

Boiled Brisket with Dumplings

To make: 15 minutes plus soaking   **To cook:** see method   **Serves: see below**

corned beef brisket*
mixed vegetables, e.g. onions,
    carrots, turnips
pepper or peppercorns
For the dumplings:
1 cup self-rising flour or all-purpose
    flour with 1 teaspoon baking
    powder
pinch salt
¼ cup ground beef suet
water to mix
*Allow 6–8 oz. uncooked meat per
person.
Quick tip:
A pressure cooker is an ideal way of cooking brisket and beef tongue. Soak the salted meat overnight as described in the method. Put the meat with any vegetables required to flavor the stock and meat into the pressure cooker. Bring up to 15 lb. pressure and allow 7 minutes per pound for prime meat or 10 minutes per pound for the less tender brisket. Allow to drop to room temperature.
To economize:
Allow less meat and add soaked navy beans to the liquid.

Soak the meat overnight in cold water to cover. This is very important as the meat can be spoiled by being too salty. Put into a pan with fresh water to cover. If cooking a very large piece of beef, you may want to add the vegetables at the end of the cooking period so they have good shape and flavor; for a smaller piece of meat put them in at the beginning. Bring the liquid to a boil, then lower the heat and simmer gently, adding pepper or peppercorns to taste. Allow nearly 35 minutes per pound and 35 minutes additional, as brisket is a firm-textured meat that needs plenty of cooking. To make the dumplings, sift the flour or flour and baking powder with the salt. Cut in shortening until particles are very fine. Add enough water to make a slightly sticky dough. Form into about 8 small balls with floured fingers and put into the boiling liquid (always check there is plenty of liquid before cooking dumplings). Simmer for 15–20 minutes until well risen and light.

To serve:
Hot with the vegetables and dumplings; allow the remainder of the meat to cool in the liquid, see the top of the opposite page.

To vary:
Cook the meat in hard cider instead of water; this is particularly good with tongue.

Add chopped mixed herbs to the flour in the dumplings.

Pressed beef tongue: Soak beef tongue overnight in cold water to cover. Cook as the brisket above, allowing 30 minutes per pound and 30 minutes additional. Allow the tongue to cool sufficiently to handle, then remove from the liquid. Skin and remove all the tiny bones and gristle. Roll up into a round and press into a cake pan or round mold; it should be a fairly tight fit. Boil the liquid until reduced to not much more than 1¼ cups. Mix 2 teaspoons unflavored gelatin with 3 tablespoons cold water. Stir into the hot liquid and continue stirring until dissolved. Strain the liquid over the tongue, put a saucer and weight on top and chill until firm. Unmold and serve with a salad. This is sufficient for 12–18 good portions.

Calf tongues and lamb tongues can be cooked in the same way, but these are rarely sold pre-salted, so soaking overnight is unnecessary. Cook the tongues with salt and pepper to taste until tender, skin and proceed as under beef tongue, pressing the meat into a neat shape. These smaller tongues are excellent served hot with some of the stock used to make a gravy.

Buying Economical Meat

Although there is a good selection of dishes for special occasions, you will also find plenty of practical and money-saving ideas using meat in this section.

When you want to save money, chose some of the less expensive meats, e.g., chuck steak, neck or shoulder of lamb or buy ground beef. A casserole in which both meat and vegetables are cooked together in the oven, is one of the most practical dishes.

To make a casserole:
Choose a strong, deep ovenproof dish with a lid. Put layers of well seasoned meat, sliced raw potatoes and onions into the dish. Add enough liquid to half cover the ingredients and always end with sliced, seasoned potatoes.

Try:
Shoulder lamb chops, flavored with finely chopped mint and use cider as the liquid.

Diced bacon slices mixed with diced lean boneless pork. Flavor with chopped mixed herbs and use beer as the liquid.

To cook a casserole:
Top the sliced potatoes with a little margarine or fat; make sure the lid does not press down on this, as it would stick. Cover the casserole and bake for at least 2 hours in slow to very moderate oven, 300–325°F. Remove the lid for the last 30 minutes so potatoes become crisp and brown.

Interesting New Stews

Italian beef stew:
Follow the recipe for Savory Beef Stew on page 71, but use half stock and half red wine. Add 1–2 teaspoons chopped fresh or ¼ teaspoon dried rosemary and 3 tablespoons tomato paste.

Boeuf flamande:
Follow the recipe for Savory Beef Stew on page 71, but use half stock and half beer. Do not use carrots or turnips in the stew, but add ⅔ cup dried prunes and/or apricots.

Lamb in fruit sauce:
Follow the recipe for Spring Lamb on page 71, but omit the lima beans and add 2–3 peeled, cored and thickly sliced apples and several tablespoons seedless raisins for the last 30 minutes of the cooking time.

Curried Stuffed Peppers

To make: 20 minutes   **To cook:** 50 minutes   **Serves 4**

4 medium-sized green peppers
salt
For the filling:
1 onion
¼ cup fat
¼ cup flour
1 tablespoon curry powder
2 cups stock or water and 2 beef bouillon cubes
salt and pepper
12 oz. ground chuck
bouquet garni (see page 28)
Quick tip:
Use canned stewing steak and flavor with a little curry powder.

Cut the tops off the peppers. Remove the seeds and put the prepared peppers and tops on one side. Chop the onion and sauté this in the hot fat for 2–3 minutes, then stir in the flour and curry powder and cook for several minutes. Mix in the stock or water and bouillon cubes gradually, then bring to a boil and cook for 3 minutes, stirring continuously. Add the salt, pepper, ground chuck and bouquet garni. Simmer gently for 40 minutes, stirring from time to time. Remove the bouquet garni. Meanwhile blanch the peppers and tops, i.e. put into boiling salted water, bring the water to a boil again and simmer for 5 minutes only, then drain.

To serve:
Fill the hot peppers with the hot curried mixture, put the tops on and serve on a heated dish. The combination of the firm peppers and the curry mixture is delicious.

To vary:
To give a soft texture to the peppers, brush the stuffed peppers with melted fat or butter and bake for 20–25 minutes in a moderately hot oven 375–400°F.

To freeze:
Freeze, then wrap and use within 6 weeks.

To economize:
Use the stuffing above in or with cheaper vegetables, i.e. halves of cooked zucchini scooped out, cooked large Spanish onions, hollowed out.

Hamburger

Hamburgers

To make: 10 minutes   **To cook:** 10 minutes   **Serves 4**

2 onions
1 lb. ground chuck or round
2 egg yolks or 1 egg
salt and pepper or seasoned salt
few drops Worcestershire sauce
   (optional)
little flour (see method)
To fry:
little fat
2 tomatoes
4 hamburger buns
Quick tip:
Use instant minced onion instead of fresh.

Cut the onions into rings, then finely chop two or three rings to give 3 tablespoons. Add to the beef with the egg yolks or egg, salt and pepper and Worcestershire sauce, if using. Mix well, then form into four flat cakes on a very lightly floured surface. Heat the fat in a fairly large frying pan and add the meat cakes to the pan with the remaining onion rings. Fry the hamburgers for about 10 minutes, turning once. Stir the onions several times during cooking. Slice the tomatoes and add to the pan about 3 minutes before the hamburgers are cooked. Split the buns and toast lightly, place on one half a layer of onion rings, the hamburger, and tomato slices. Top with the other half of the bun.

To serve:
Hot with French fries or potato chips and salad.

To vary:
See to economize. It is not essential to add the egg yolks or egg, but it helps to bind the meat together so that it does not break up during frying. This makes the mixture softer to handle so flour your hands.

To freeze:
These freeze better before cooking. Prepare, separate with plastic wrap or foil and freeze. Use within 3 months. Cook from the frozen state. It is also an excellent idea to keep buns in the freezer, see page 148.

To economize:
Use supermarket ground beef. Omit egg and bind with a little milk or grated raw potato. Add a few breadcrumbs to make the meat go further.

Sweet and sour meat balls

Sweet & Sour Meat Balls

To make: 25 minutes   **To cook:** 30 minutes   **Serves 6**

1½ lbs. ground beef or pork
1 clove garlic
½ cup flour
½ cup soft breadcrumbs
salt and pepper
1 egg, beaten
To fry:
6 tablespoons lard
For the sauce:
½ cup sugar
½ cup vinegar
⅓ cup soy sauce
3 tablespoons cornstarch
2 cups water
1 green pepper
12 oz. tomatoes
1 can crushed pineapple
Quick tip:
Use frozen hamburgers and fry these, then heat in the sweet and sour sauce.

Mix together the meat, crushed garlic, half the flour, the breadcrumbs and salt and pepper. Mix with the egg and form into balls (this quantity should make about 30 balls). Roll the meat balls in the remaining flour. Melt the lard and fry the balls in batches, allowing about 10 minutes for each batch; turn frequently during cooking. Keep each batch hot when cooked. Meanwhile prepare the sauce. Place the sugar, vinegar and soy sauce in a pan. Stir in the cornstarch with a little of the measured water and add to the pan with the remaining water. Bring to a boil, stirring, and simmer for 5 minutes. Cut the pepper into strips (discard seeds), skin and chop the tomatoes and drain the pineapple well. Add to the sauce and simmer for 5–10 minutes. When the meat balls are cooked, divide between 2 large frying pans, pour the sauce over them and simmer gently for 3 minutes. Serve with noodles.
To vary:
Do not make meat balls, but dice tender fillet or other prime steak, pork, lamb or cooked lobster meat. Sauté in hot butter then heat in the sauce.
To freeze:
The meat balls may be prepared then frozen. Fry from the frozen state. Use within 2–3 months. The sauce is better freshly made.
To economize:
Use inexpensive chuck steak, cooked until tender and diced.

Beef Stuffed Crêpes

To make: 25 minutes   **To cook:** 1 hour   **Serves 4–6**

For the filling:
1 onion
2 carrots
¼ cup drippings or fat
1 lb. ground beef
1¼ cups stock or water and 1 bouillon
  cube
½–1 tablespoon tomato paste
salt and pepper
1 tablespoon flour
For the crêpes:
1 cup all-purpose flour
¼ teaspoon salt
1 large egg
1¼ cups milk or milk and water
To fry:
fat or oil

Chop the peeled onion and grate the peeled carrots. Melt the drippings or fat in a pan and fry the ground beef and onion together, browning gently for 10 minutes. Add the grated carrots, most of the stock or water and bouillon cube, tomato paste and salt and pepper. Simmer for 30 minutes until tender. Skim off the excess fat. Mix the flour with the remaining stock or water until smooth and add to the ingredients in the pan. Bring to a boil and simmer until it becomes a thick mixture. Make the crêpe batter as page 137. Cook the crêpes until golden brown on either side and keep hot. Fill each crêpe with a portion of the beef mixture and roll up. Arrange in an ovenproof dish, cover lightly with foil and bake in a moderately hot oven, 375–400°F. for 15–20 minutes.
To vary:
Chicken crêpes: Blend cooked minced or diced chicken with a white sauce, see page 54, or use minced uncooked chicken in the recipe above.
To freeze:
Add 2 teaspoons oil to the crêpe batter. Freeze. Use within 6 weeks.

Speedy Moussaka

To make: 25 minutes **To cook:** 1–1½ hours **Serves 4–6**

2 onions
6 tablespoons fat
¼ cup flour
1¼ cups stock or water and 1 bouillon
cube
1 lb. ground beef or lamb
salt and pepper
good pinch fines herbes
1 lb. peeled potatoes
1 eggplant
1¼ cups evaporated milk
1½ cups grated cheese

Peel and chop the onions, sauté in half the fat for a few minutes, then add the flour and cook for 2 or 3 minutes. Gradually stir in the stock or water and bouillon cube, bring to a boil and cook until thickened. Add the meat, stir very well to break up the lumps that form. Add salt, pepper, herbs, then bring the mixture to a boil, stir again. Lower the heat, cover the pan and allow to simmer for 35–40 minutes. Skim excess fat. Stir once or twice during the cooking, as the mixture is very thick. Meanwhile boil the potatoes in salted water until tender, drain and slice fairly thickly. Slice the unpeeled eggplant thinly and sauté in the remaining fat until tender. Put half the potatoes and half the sliced eggplant into a casserole, top with a third of the evaporated milk and cheese and salt and pepper. Add the meat mixture, another third of the milk and cheese and salt and pepper, then the rest of the eggplant and potato slices. Pour the remainder of the milk over the top very carefully and sprinkle with the last of the cheese. Salt and pepper the mixture and bake for 30 minutes in a moderate oven, 350–375°F.

To serve:
With salad or green vegetables. This makes an excellent dish for a buffet supper.

To vary:
Make a cheese sauce with 2 tablespoons margarine, ¼ cup flour, 2 cups milk, salt and pepper and 1½ cups (6 oz.) grated Swiss or Gruyère cheese. Use instead of the evaporated milk and cheese. Add an egg to the evaporated milk or the cheese sauce.

To freeze:
Cook, freeze, then cover well. Use within 3 months.

To economize:
Use leftover beef and omit the first stage. Mix beef with 1–2 tablespoons instant minced onion and allow it to stand for 30 minutes to improve the flavor. Make the sauce as the recipe, stir in the cooked meat, season and add herbs, then use. Grate leftover pieces of rather dry cheese.

Speedy moussaka

Cooking Variety Meats

Variety meats embrace a wide range of very nutritious meats. Most of them are highly perishable, so store carefully after purchase and use as soon as possible, unless you plan to freeze them.
To freeze variety meats:
Most variety meats should be eaten within 3 months.

Fried Sweetbreads

To make: 20 minutes plus soaking   **To cook:** 25 minutes   **Serves 4**

1 lb. lamb or calf sweetbreads
1¼ cups chicken stock or water and 1
  chicken bouillon cube
juice of ½ a lemon
salt and pepper
To coat:
¼ cup flour
1 egg
3 tablespoons water
1 cup crisp dry breadcrumbs
To fry:
oil or butter and oil, see method
To garnish:
lemon slices
Quick tip:
Put crumbs into a bag, drop the sweetbreads into the bag. Shake vigorously.

Soak the sweetbreads in cold water for at least 1 hour. Drain then put into a pan with fresh cold water to cover. Bring the water to a boil, throw this away. This is known as "blanching" the sweetbreads and it whitens them. Return the sweetbreads to the pan with the stock or water and bouillon cube, lemon juice and salt and pepper. Simmer for 10–15 minutes. Lift the sweetbreads from the liquid; this could be used as the basis for a brown sauce, see page 82, to serve with the sweetbreads. Allow the meat to cool and drain well, remove skin and gristle. Coat the sweetbreads in flour mixed with salt and pepper. Beat the egg with the water, brush the sweetbreads with this, then coat in the crumbs. Either fry in hot deep oil at 360°F. for 5–6 minutes or shallow fry in a mixture of butter and oil (use about ¼ cup butter and 1 tablespoon oil). Turn the sweetbreads as they shallow fry. Drain on absorbent paper.
To serve:
Garnished with lemon slices and with brown sauce, as page 82, or tartar sauce, page 55.
To vary:
Coat the sweetbreads in crushed herb stuffing mix in place of crumbs.
To freeze:
The sweetbreads can be prepared ready for frying, i.e. coated with egg and crumbs, then frozen on a flat tray and wrapped. Use within 6 weeks and fry from the frozen state.
To economize:
Sweetbreads are expensive, so serve small portions with plenty of vegetables.

Fried sweetbreads

Oxtail Ragoût

⅔ cup navy or pea beans
salt and pepper
1 large or 2 smaller oxtail
¼ cup fat
1 lb. mixed vegetables, e.g. onions, celery, carrots
½ cup flour
5 cups water
bouquet garni (see page 28)
Quick tip:
Use canned beans.

To make: 30 minutes plus soaking   **To cook:** 2½–3 hours   **Serves 4–6**

Put the beans to soak overnight in cold water to cover. Next day simmer in fresh water with salt and pepper to taste, for about 2 hours or until tender. Meanwhile slice oxtail in 2-inch chunks and brown in the hot fat for a few minutes, lift out of the pan. Prepare the vegetables and sauté a small amount in any fat remaining in the pan. Stir in the flour, then stir in the water and bring to a boil. Cook until slightly thickened. Return the oxtail to the pan, add salt and pepper and bouquet garni. Cover the pan and simmer for about 1½ hours, add the rest of the vegetables and continue cooking until nearly tender. Add the cooked, well drained beans about 15–20 minutes before serving. Serve with a green vegetable. If preferred cool, skim off the surplus fat, then reheat.
To freeze:
This dish can be frozen, but is slightly disappointing, as the oxtail loses its rich flavor. Use within 3–4 weeks.
To economize:
Increase the amount of beans.

Liver Risotto

3–4 tablespoons oil
2 onions
4 oz. mushrooms
2–3 tomatoes
1 cup long grain or Italian rice
2 cups stock or water and 2 chicken bouillon cubes
8 oz. chicken, calf or lamb liver
3 tablespoons raisins
salt and pepper
1–2 tablespoons chopped parsley
grated Parmesan cheese

To make: 15 minutes   **To cook:** 25 minutes   **Serves 4–6**

Heat the oil in the pan and fry the chopped onions, chopped mushrooms and tomatoes. Add the rice and stir into the hot vegetable mixture (this prevents it becoming sticky). Add the stock or water and bouillon cubes, and simmer for 10 minutes, stirring once or twice as the mixture thickens. Add the diced liver, raisins, salt, pepper and parsley. Continue cooking for a further 10 minutes until the excess liquid has evaporated and rice is tender.
To serve:
Top with the grated cheese.
To vary:
Seafood Risotto: Use shellfish instead of diced liver, add towards the end of the cooking time, omit the raisins if wished.
To freeze:
Although better eaten freshly made, this dish can be frozen for 1 month. See comments on page 96 about freezing rice mixtures.

Braised Kidneys

12 lamb kidneys
¼ cup fat
1¼ cups Espagnole sauce (see page 82)
Tabasco
To garnish:
parsley

To make: 20 minutes   **To cook:** 20 minutes   **Serves 4**

Remove membranes from kidneys, then fry these in the hot fat. Pour over the Espagnole sauce and flavor with a few drops of Tabasco. Cover and simmer for 15 minutes or until tender.
To serve:
As a substantial hors d'oeuvre on buttered toast, with mixed vegetables or as a filling for omelets, see page 124. Garnish with parsley.
To vary:
Use economical diced beef kidney with double the amount of sauce, simmer for 1½ hours. Serve with potatoes, rice or noodles.
To freeze:
Cook and cool, then cover and freeze. Use within 1 month.
To economize:
See To vary.

Fried Liver & Bacon

1 lb. lamb or calf liver
1 tablespoon flour
salt and pepper
¼ cup fat, or butter, or mix butter and fat or drippings
4 slices bacon
2–4 tomatoes

To make: 5 minutes   **To cook:** 10 minutes   **Serves 4**

Coat the slices of liver with a little flour mixed with salt and pepper, do not use too much. Heat the fat or butter or mixture of fats and fry the liver for 1–2 minutes then turn and fry on the other side. Add the bacon slices and halved seasoned tomatoes during cooking. Do NOT overcook the liver, otherwise it becomes tough. Serve as soon as possible.
To vary:
If you like gravy with liver, use the drippings in the frying pan so the gravy has the taste of the liver, bacon and tomatoes.

Accompaniments to Meat & Poultry

Some Gravies for Meat & Poultry

Many poultry and meat dishes depend upon a good sauce or stuffing to make them interesting. While there are certain basic, or traditional stuffings and sauces that are served with certain meats or poultry, do not be too conservative. Be prepared to try new ideas to give a change of flavor to an old favorite.

Many of the most familiar sauces which are based upon a white sauce are found on page 54. Bread and cranberry sauces to serve with chicken and turkey are on page 88 as well as several sauces to blend with duckling or goose. The most important sauce for meat is a gravy.

To make good gravy:
If roasting meat you can make the gravy in either the roasting pan or in a saucepan. If making in a roasting pan, pour out all the fat except about 1 tablespoon. For a thin gravy: Blend a very little flour into the fat (use only 1 tablespoon) and stir over low heat. Gradually add up to 1¼ cups meat stock, or strained water from cooking vegetables. Bring slowly to a boil and cook until clear. Flavor with salt and pepper. Add browning sauce for color. Increase the amount of flour for a thicker gravy.

Brown sauce:
Try to use a good flavored dripping for this sauce. Heat ¼ cup drippings (or fat) in a pan, add 1 chopped onion and a small piece of carrot and sauté in the hot fat. Stir in ¼ cup flour, cook gently for 2–3 minutes then blend in 1¼ cups stock or water and a beef or chicken bouillon cube. Bring to a boil, stir until thickened, strain or sieve, then season and reheat. This sauce can be flavored with Madeira or port wine.

Mint sauce:
Mix finely chopped mint leaves with vinegar and sugar to taste.

Apple sauce:
Many meats and poultry are improved with a fruit sauce and apple sauce blends particularly well with pork and duck. Simmer peeled sliced cooking apples in a little water with sugar or honey to sweeten. Sieve or purée in blender or food mill until smooth. This freezes well.

Horseradish cream:
Grate a small horseradish and blend with lightly whipped cream. Season and flavor with a little prepared mustard, lemon juice or vinegar and a pinch of sugar.

Horseradish sauce:
Make a white sauce as page 54, remove from the heat and stir in a little grated fresh horseradish, prepared mustard and lemon juice or vinegar. Do not boil again.

Parsley sauce:
Although this is often served with vegetables or fish, it is also a good accompaniment to boiled ham. Make a sauce with 2 tablespoons butter or margarine, ¼ cup flour and 1¼ cups milk or half milk and half ham stock (use fish stock or vegetable water when appropriate). Stir until thickened, as white sauce, page 54, then add salt and pepper and 1–2 tablespoons chopped parsley. Heat for 1–2 minutes only.

Some Stuffings for Meat & Poultry

An interesting stuffing adds flavor to all kinds of meat and poultry.

Apple and onion stuffing:
Peel, core and dice 4 large cooking apples and dice 4 large onions. Mix with ¼ cup melted butter or margarine, 1 tablespoon brown sugar, 2 cups soft breadcrumbs or mashed potato and season with salt and pepper. Use for duck, goose and pork. If cooking in a separate dish cover well and bake 1 hour in a moderate oven, 350°F. The recipe for Sage and Onion Stuffing is on page 89.

Roast beef

Chestnut Stuffing

To make: 15–30 minutes   **To cook:** see method   **Serves 4–6**

2 lbs. chestnuts or 1 can (15 oz.)
  natural chestnut purée
little stock or water
salt and pepper
4 oz. chopped ham or bacon
¼ cup melted butter
3 tablespoons chopped parsley

If using fresh chestnuts, split the skins, boil for 10 minutes, then remove the skins while warm. Return the nuts to the stock or seasoned water and simmer until tender then purée through a sieve or food mill or blender. Mix the fresh or canned purée with the remaining ingredients. Use as a stuffing for chicken, turkey or duck.

To vary:
If stuffing duck add 1–2 chopped fresh onions and a little sage.

To freeze:
This freezes well, use within 3 months.

To economize:
Mix with 2 cups soft breadcrumbs or 1 lb. bulk sausage.

Veal (Parsley & Thyme) Stuffing

To make: 15 minutes   **To cook:** see method   **Serves 4–6**

2 cups soft breadcrumbs
¼ cup shredded suet or melted butter
  or margarine
grated rind and juice of ½ a lemon
1–2 tablespoons chopped parsley
½–1 teaspoon chopped lemon thyme
  or ¼ teaspoon dried thyme
salt and pepper
1 egg, beaten

Mix all the ingredients together. This stuffing is excellent with chicken, turkey, veal, etc. You will need at least twice the quantity for a turkey. Put into the neck end and the body cavity of a bird. This stuffing can be rolled into small balls and baked for about 35 minutes in a moderate oven, 350°F.

To vary:
Add a little finely chopped raw bacon, or the chopped cooked giblets of the bird or mix with 8 oz. bulk sausage.

To freeze:
Pack into a carton or plastic bag, use within 3 months.

83

Poultry and Game

Choose poultry carefully. Young birds have pliable wishbones and the legs and breast are plump and pliable, not sinewy. A fricassee fowl is a creamy color, but there should not be too much fat. Duck and geese generally have little breast meat, but buy one with as much flesh on the breast and legs as possible. Avoid over-fat ducks and geese. Poultry should have a fresh smell.

For frying or broiling, buy fryers or broilers, small and plump. For roasting buy a larger young chicken or capon. Fricassee fowl can be cooked slowly in a casserole or steamed or boiled. If substituting an older fricassee fowl for a chicken in casserole recipes, allow about twice the cooking time and increase the amount of liquid slightly.

Ducks and geese are less adaptable and are best roasted and used in casseroles, see page 94.

Economical poultry and game dishes: Use small pieces of cooked poultry as a filling in crêpes or in omelets.

Sauté fairly solid pieces of cooked poultry in a little hot butter then place pieces into a Yorkshire pudding batter and make a poultry "Toad in the Hole", see the recipe on page 99.

Really young tender rabbit can be fried like young chicken. Coat the pieces in seasoned flour, then in beaten egg and dry bread or cracker crumbs. Fry fairly quickly to brown the outside, then lower the heat and cook slowly until tender. Drain the rabbit on absorbent paper and serve with tartar sauce, as the recipe on page 55, and garnished with wedges of lemon.

The coating for the rabbit pieces can be flavored with a little grated lemon rind or chopped herbs.

To freeze: Poultry and game are successful foods to freeze, as indicated by the popularity of commercial products. When freezing poultry or game birds yourself, check that they are fresh, cleaned and trussed. Wrap the giblets in a separate plastic bag, put this inside or near the birds. Cover the sharp leg bones with extra plastic wrap or foil so they do not pierce the wrapping. Wrap several layers of plastic wrap or foil as tightly as possible round the birds. The tighter the wrapping, the more the air is excluded; this hastens freezing and preserves flavor and gives the best result. Fresh game should be hung to taste before freezing.

Frozen whole birds or large pieces of game meat should be defrosted before cooking. This takes a surprisingly long time. A good-sized chicken needs at least 24 hours in the refrigerator to thaw out properly; a large turkey takes from 48–82 hours. The reason it is important to allow the flesh to thaw out is that it is surprisingly easy to cook the outer flesh of poultry or game birds while still frozen, but the heat may not penetrate through to the inside of the carcass. Small portions of frozen chicken, such as breast or legs, can generally be cooked from the frozen state, if more convenient. There are exceptions to this, e.g. when coating the pieces or when they need to absorb extra flavor. This is indicated in the recipes in this book. Frozen rabbit and hare pieces can also be cooked without defrosting.

Store frozen chicken for up to a year, I prefer to use within 8 months. Duck, goose and turkey: use within 5–6 months. Game birds: freeze for up to 8 months, game meat for 6 months. When cooked, halve these times or store according to the dish.

Deviled chicken legs

Deviled Chicken Legs

To make: 10 minutes   **To cook:** 16–20 minutes   **Serves 4**

For the deviled sauce:
¼ cup olive or corn oil
1 tablespoon Worcestershire sauce
1 tablespoon tarragon vinegar
1 tablespoon finely chopped onion or
    1 teaspoon instant minced onion
1 teaspoon French mustard
salt and pepper

4 chicken legs
8 oz. mushrooms
1 tablespoon olive or corn oil
To garnish:
parsley
Quick tip:
A good way to heat ready-cooked chicken or turkey. Allow 2–3 minutes on either side.

Mix all the ingredients for the sauce together, adding salt and pepper to taste. If using frozen chicken pieces, allow these to thaw out first. Score the chicken legs with a sharp knife and place in broiler pan. Brush with the deviled sauce and place under hot broiler. Broil for 8–10 minutes, basting frequently with the sauce. Turn, brush with more sauce and continue broiling for a further 8–10 minutes, or until cooked. Brush the mushrooms with the oil, add to broiler pan for the last 5 minutes cooking time.

To serve:
Hot, garnished with parsley and with salad.
To vary:
Add ½–1 teaspoon curry powder to the sauce. Cook lamb chops in the same way.
To freeze:
Do not freeze this dish, but you can use frozen chicken.
To economize:
Make chicken rissoles with ⅔ cup thick white sauce, see page 54, 1–2 cups ground cooked chicken (grind skin and all the tiny pieces), 1 cup soft breadcrumbs and salt and pepper. Make into flat cakes, sauté in hot butter until brown on both sides. Pour the deviled sauce above over cakes and heat for 2–3 minutes only.

Chicken Cordon Bleu

To make: 10 minutes   **To cook:** 12–15 minutes   **Serves 4**

4 chicken breasts
4 slices ham
4 slices Gruyère cheese
salt and pepper
2 tablespoons flour
To coat:
1 egg
1 cup soft breadcrumbs
To fry:
deep oil or fat
Quick tip:
Use ready-cooked chicken breasts. Insert ham and cheese, coat and heat for 2–3 minutes only.

If using frozen chicken breasts allow them to defrost for the recipe. Dry well, then slit to make a pocket. Insert the slices of ham and cheese into the pockets. Mix a little salt and pepper with the flour and dust the chicken breasts with this. Coat in beaten egg and crumbs and fry slowly in the oil or fat until crisp, golden brown and tender on all sides. This takes about 12–15 minutes. Drain on absorbent paper. Serve at once with salad.

To vary:
Chicken Rossini: Fill the chicken breasts with pâté and finely diced uncooked mushrooms instead of the ham and cheese. Coat and fry as above.

Russian chicken: Blend a little prepared mustard with ¼ cup butter. Add 1 tablespoon finely chopped onion, 1 tablespoon finely diced green pepper and 3 tablespoons thinly sliced mushrooms. Press this mixture into the chicken breasts, then coat and fry as above.

Chicken in sour cream sauce: Do not coat or fill the chicken breasts. Simply fry until golden brown in a little butter. Lift out of the pan, add some finely diced onion and mushrooms and sauté for 2–3 minutes. Pour in 1¼ cups sour cream and season with salt and pepper. Replace the chicken breasts and heat gently until tender. Do not boil.
To freeze:
The completed dish is not suitable for freezing, but it is a good idea to prepare this dish, then freeze. Fry from the frozen state and use within 2 months.
To economize:
Use crumbled crisp bacon and grated cheese as the filling.

To Broil Chicken

Cut chicken into pieces as below. Brush with melted butter or oil. Put on the oiled or greased grid of the broiler pan. Place under a hot broiler 6–8 inches away from source of heat and broil slowly until brown on either side. Some of the suggestions for adding flavor to broiled or fried meat on page 61 would also be suitable for chicken.

To Fry Chicken

Buy cut-up broiler-fryers or cut into halves or quarters. For shallow frying, heat fat, oil or butter and oil to give a depth of ½ inch. Fry quickly to brown the chicken on either side, lower the heat and fry slowly until chicken is tender.

The chicken can be coated with flour mixed with salt and pepper, beaten egg and crumbs as recipe above or batter, page 44, then fried in shallow or deep fat. Drain on absorbent paper and serve hot or cold with vegetables or salad.

Chicken cordon bleu

To Roast Chicken & Turkey

Both chicken and turkey have the same tendency to dry during cooking, unless kept well covered with fat. Bacon can be used to cover the breast of the bird, but also butter, margarine or chicken fat; meat drippings have too pronounced a flavor. Stuffings inside a bird give extra flavor and also help to keep it moist. If you want to roast a bird without stuffing, then place a large piece of butter inside to keep it from drying.

A covered roasting pan is ideal for these birds or put the bird covered with butter or other fat into the pan, see above, then lay foil loosely over. I prefer this to wrapping the bird in foil. The modern plastic cooking bags are also excellent for keeping the moist texture and allowing the bird to brown slowly. When using a covered roasting pan, foil or bag, allow 10–15 minutes extra cooking time, or use 25°F. higher than when using an open roasting pan. If you choose to wrap the bird entirely in foil, then allow at least 15 minutes extra cooking time.

There are three ways of roasting poultry. These depend upon the weight of the bird so stuff the bird and weigh after trussing.

1) Fast roasting:
Allow 15 minutes per lb. and 15 minutes additional up to 12 lbs. After this add an extra 12 minutes only for each extra lb. Use a hot oven, 425°F. for the first 30–45 minutes, then lower the heat to moderately hot, 375–400°F. for the rest of the time. This is suitable for fresh birds that have not been frozen.

2) Slower roasting:
Allow 25 minutes per lb. and 25 minutes additional, plus an extra 20–22 minutes per lb. over 12 lbs. The extra 2 minutes for large birds is good if the turkey has been frozen. Use a moderate oven, 325–350°F. This method is far better for defrosted frozen birds, or if you feel the bird is not quite as perfect as you would wish.

3) Ultra slow roasting:
This appeals to many people who have bought a very large bird and want to roast it during the night. Allow 1½ hours for the first lb., then 25 minutes for every extra lb. up to 12 lbs., then reduce the time to 20–22 minutes per extra lb. Set the oven to 275–300°F. The skin does not look very crisp and appetizing with this method, so raise the temperature to 350°F. for the last 20–30 minutes.

To Roast Portions of Turkey

Make the stuffing in the usual way. Press this against the cut side of the bird and lay stuffing side down in the roasting pan. It is quite a good idea to place a piece of foil under the stuffing as this makes it easier to remove from the pan. Cover if wished, see above. Time the roasting as for the whole bird, but tend to shorten the time by a few minutes, as it is easier for the heat to penetrate through part of a bird.

Using Frozen Poultry or Game

It is always rather surprising just how long it takes to defrost a frozen chicken, duck, goose or turkey. Allow at least 24 hours for a small bird and up to 72 hours for a very large turkey. Do not try to cook from the frozen state, but if you want to hurry defrosting put the bird into cold, BUT NOT HOT, water, or into a microwave oven.

After defrosting, dry the bird very well, both inside and out. Remember that often the giblets are packed inside the bird, take these out and put them into a pan. Cover with water, add salt and pepper and simmer to give you a really good stock for gravy.

To Serve with Chicken & Turkey

The traditional accompaniments to chicken and turkey are:

Bacon rolls:
Stretch thick-sliced bacon by stroking with a knife; this makes it easier to roll the bacon. Roll slices firmly and spear on skewers. Either bake in the oven for the last 15–25 minutes of the roasting time, depending upon the heat of the oven, or broil until crisp. You can roll the bacon around sausages and bake or broil these together.

Sausages:
Bake around the bird or in a separate pan in the oven.

Bread sauce:
Peel a small onion and press in 3–4 whole cloves (omit these if wished). Put the onion into a pan with 1¼ cups milk, ¼ cup butter or margarine, 1 cup soft breadcrumbs and salt and pepper. Bring the milk to a boil, cover the pan and put on one side, in a warm place if possible. Leave until almost ready to serve the meal, then heat gently, stirring well. Remove the onion, beat hard, then serve. This is enough for 4–6.

It improves the flavor of bread sauce if you add 1½–3 tablespoons heavy cream before reheating. Bread sauce has a tendency to burn, so try cooking it in a pan set over hot water, or the top part of a double boiler. Alternatively bring the sauce to a boil, transfer to a dish, cover and keep warm.

Cranberry sauce:
This is the traditional sauce for turkey. Simmer 4 cups fresh cranberries with 2 cups sugar and 1 cup water, flavoring this with grated rind of 1 orange or ½ cup port wine. When just tender remove from the heat and press through a sieve or food mill. Chill until firm.

A delicious relish is made by grinding 4 cups raw cranberries with 2 small oranges, quartered. Stir in 1½ cups sugar. Chill.

To freeze:
Both the bread sauce and the cranberry relish freeze well. Use the bread sauce within about 6 weeks, but the cranberry relish lasts up to 1 year.

Veal (parsley and thyme) and chestnut stuffing are excellent with chicken and turkey and these recipes are on page 83.

To Roast Duck & Goose

These birds have a generous amount of fat and it is important to encourage most of this to run out during cooking. Duck and goose are also much improved if the skin is crisp and brown. The way to achieve perfect roasting is to prick duckling all over once or twice during cooking and goose several times. Do this very lightly using a fork so the fat "spurts out" and does not soak into the flesh.

Use an open roasting pan and time as for roasting chicken or turkey, page 87. If you have a rack stand the bird on this in the roasting pan; do not add extra fat. Follow the roasting times for chicken or turkey on page 87.

To Serve with Duck & Goose

These birds have a rich flavor and therefore all accompaniments should be well flavored, preferably with fruit. Apple sauce, page 82, and sage and onion stuffing, below, are traditional, but there are other stuffings and sauces to serve with either bird.

Goose stuffed with prunes and apples:
Stuff the bird with pitted prunes and quartered cored apples sprinkled with a little sage.

Caneton aux cerises (Duckling with cherries):
This is ideal for small young ducklings (allow half per person) rather than the larger ducks. Follow the roasting instructions opposite, but do not stuff. Simmer the giblets to give a good stock, then strain. To make a sauce for 6–8 people, pour 1¼ cups giblet stock, 1¼ cups cherry syrup from canned dark sweet Bing cherries, blended with 4 tablespoons cornstarch into a pan. Stir over low heat until thickened, add 3 tablespoons redcurrant jelly, 3 tablespoons cherry brandy and 2 cups well drained cherries. Heat gently. This sauce does not need fat. Halve the ducklings and serve topped with sauce.

Caneton à l'orange (Duckling with orange sauce):
To make enough sauce for 4 people, cut the rind from 2 navel oranges, remove the white part, cut colored part into matchstick pieces. Soak in water to cover for 1–2 hours then simmer in 2 cups strained giblet stock until the rind is tender. Do not cover the pan so the liquid evaporates a little. Mix ⅔ cup orange juice with 2 tablespoons cornstarch, put into the pan with the stock and simmer until thickened and clear. Add salt and pepper and 1 teaspoon sugar.

This sauce is varied in many ways; you can flavor a good gravy with orange juice and a little Curaçao (orange-flavored brandy). Another method is just to simmer large pieces of rind or even grated rind in the stock until it is reduced to about 1¼ cups, then strain and use with the juice in the recipe above.

Sage and onion stuffing:
Peel and chop 4 large onions. Simmer in 1¼ cups water with salt and pepper for 10 minutes. Strain (reserve stock) and mix onions with 3 cups soft breadcrumbs, ½–1 tablespoon chopped fresh sage or 1 teaspoon dried sage and ½ cup ground beef suet or melted butter or margarine. Stir in reserved onion stock or 1–2 eggs. Stuff duck or goose, sew or skewer openings and roast as usual. This stuffing can also be cooked separately in a covered dish for 1 hour with the duck or goose. Serves 4.

To Roast Game

In order to judge whether game is sufficiently young to roast, rather than cook in a stew, check to see the legs are plump and not sinewy. While there may be some fat on a young bird, a thick layer of fat under the skin generally indicates an older bird, more suitable for cooking in a casserole dish. Frozen game should be thawed in refrigerator before cooking.

If you like fresh game with a strong flavor hang for more than a week before cooking, otherwise hang for a few days only; if cooked when freshly killed the meat tends to be tough.

All game tends to become dry when roasted unless you keep it well basted with fat.

While it is not traditional to stuff game birds, I always put in a generous piece of butter or cream cheese to make sure I moisten from the inside as well as the outside.

Roasting times:
Small birds: Partridge, pigeon, woodcock need a total of about 25–30 minutes in a hot oven, 400°F.
Larger birds: Grouse, pheasant, etc., roast as chicken, page 87.
Young hare: Roast back sections (saddle) as pork, page 67. Casserole legs.
Young rabbit or venison: Roast as pork, page 67.

To cook older game:
Simmer gently for the time given for "boiled" chicken, page 91; then cut into pieces and put into the ragoût on page 94. 1–2 tablespoons redcurrant jelly would improve the flavor of the sauce. The Savory Beef Stew on page 71 or variations on this, page 76 can also be used as a basis for game stews.

To Serve with Roast Game

Serve game birds with bread sauce, page 88, or redcurrant jelly, fried crumbs, see below, and French fried potatoes, see below; bacon rolls are often served as well. Roast rabbit, hare and venison are generally served with the same accompaniments as pork, page 67, although you could serve the same ones as for game birds.

To fry crumbs:
Make fairly coarse breadcrumbs with your fingers (a blender makes them too fine), fry in hot butter or fat until golden brown and crisp. Drain on absorbent paper. It is worthwhile to fry a large quantity, freeze them, then pack into containers. Use within about 3 months.

French fried potatoes or Potato chips:
Cut wafer thin slices of peeled potato or ½ inch square strips of peeled potato, fry quickly in hot fat or oil, see page 104 for details of frying potatoes and testing the temperature of the oil.

Chicken Curry

To make: 25 minutes   **To cook:** 40 minutes   **Serves 4**

1 lb. boneless and skinless chicken breasts
¼ cup butter
3 onions
1 clove garlic
2 sticks celery
1 apple
1–2 tablespoons curry powder
1 tablespoon flour
1¼ cups stock or water and 1 chicken bouillon cube
salt and pepper
⅔ cup plain yogurt
1 banana
3 tablespoons chutney
To garnish:
1–2 bananas
few gherkins

Cut the chicken into cubes and fry these in the butter for a few minutes, then remove from the pan. Fry the sliced onions, crushed garlic, diced celery and peeled and diced apple in the pan drippings. Stir in the curry powder and flour. Stir in the stock or water and bouillon cube, replace the chicken and season to taste with salt and pepper. Lower the heat, cover the pan, then simmer for about 30 minutes. Stir in the yogurt, sliced banana and chutney. Cook slowly for a further 5 minutes.

To serve:
In a border of cooked rice, see page 95, garnished with bananas and gherkins and accompanied by chutney, diced pineapple and diced preserved ginger.

Note:
It is a good idea to make the curry, let it stand over-night then reheat.

To vary:
This particular recipe is delicious as a cold curry. Use diced meat in place of chicken. If using chuck steak cubes, allow 2¼ hours cooking before adding the yogurt and increase the liquid to 2 cups.

If using lamb cubes allow 1¼–1½ hours cooking and increase the liquid to 1½ cups.

To freeze:
This curry freezes well for 2 months or 3 months if the yogurt etc. is not added until the dish is reheated.

Normandy Chicken

To make: 20 minutes   **To cook:** 1 hour   **Serves 4–6**

1 chicken, 3 lbs., cut-up
2 tablespoons butter
1 tablespoon oil
1 onion
1 clove garlic
3 slices bacon
¼ cup flour
2 cups hard cider or apple juice
2 apples
⅔ cup light cream
1 tablespoon chopped parsley

Quick tip:
Make the sauce, heat diced cooked chicken in this, then add the apple and cream.

Wash chicken and pat dry. Heat the butter and oil in a large saucepan and fry the chicken on both sides until golden brown. Remove from the pan and put on a plate. Add the chopped onion, crushed garlic and chopped bacon to the fat in the pan and bake for 5 minutes, or until the onion is golden. Stir in the flour and cook for 1 minute. Gradually stir in the cider and bring to a boil; cook until thick. Return the chicken to the pan, cover and simmer gently for 30 minutes. Core and dice the apples, but do not remove the peel. Stir into the chicken mixture with the cream. Heat for 2–3 minutes WITHOUT boiling, spoon into a heated serving dish and sprinkle with chopped parsley.

To serve:
With a green salad.

To vary:
Use a little less cider and add a small amount of Calvados (apple brandy).

To freeze:
This dish does not freeze well, but frozen chicken pieces could be used; fry from the frozen state.

To economize:
Use left-over cooked meat or chicken.

Normandy chicken

To Boil Chicken

The term "boiling" is not correct in describing the way in which chicken is cooked in liquid as the liquid should only simmer gently; see comments under "to boil meat", page 74. If "boiling" a young chicken allow 20 minutes per lb. and 20 minutes additional, from the time the liquid comes to simmering point. An older boiling fowl needs 35–40 minutes per lb. and 35–40 minutes additional.

To give extra flavor to the stock and chicken, add mixed vegetables, a little wine and a bouquet garni (see page 28). Use the stock for soup and in making a sauce to serve with the bird, see parsley sauce, page 82 and sauce under Chicken Suprême, page 95.

Pies & Puddings with Poultry

Chicken and turkey lend themselves to many varying recipes for pies and puddings. The recipe below could be adapted to use pieces of turkey instead of chicken which is particularly useful now that it is possible to buy turkey parts. The recipe below using turkey in a pudding is also suitable for chicken, or see the variation on page 72.

Chicken Pie

To make: 1 hour plus standing   **To cook:** 2¼–2½ hours   **Serves 6–8**

4 lbs. roasting chicken
water
1 small onion
1 carrot
1 leek and/or 1 stick celery
salt and pepper
For the sauce:
2 onions
1–2 red peppers
1 green pepper
¼ cup butter
½ cup flour
2½ cups chicken stock (see method)
1 cup (4 oz.) grated Cheddar cheese
salt and pepper
For the pastry:
6 oz. puff pastry (see page 97)
To glaze:
1 egg
Quick tip:
Use ready cooked chicken, a can of condensed cream of chicken soup and chopped pimientos. Use 12–13 oz. frozen puff pastry.

Simmer the chicken in enough water to cover, with the vegetables and salt and pepper for about 1–1¼ hours. Remove the chicken, boil the stock until you have 2½ cups and then strain. To make the sauce, chop the onions, red pepper(s) and green pepper (discard seeds). Melt the butter in a pan, fry the onion, red and green peppers for 10 minutes. Skin and bone the chicken, cutting meat into bite-sized pieces. Place the meat in a 1½ quart casserole. Stir flour into vegetables and gradually stir in stock. Stir over heat until sauce thickens. Stir in the grated cheese but do not cook again, season to taste. Spoon sauce over the chicken and allow to cool. Roll out the puff pastry and use to cover the filled casserole. Scallop the edge and score the top of the pastry into diamonds with a knife, cutting ⅛ inch deep. Knock up the edges (see page 97) and brush with beaten egg. Bake in a very hot oven, 450°F. for 20–25 minutes. Reduce heat to moderate, 325°F. and cook for a further 30 minutes. Serve hot or cold.

To vary:
Chicken, mushroom and pepper pie: Follow the recipe above but cut the chicken into larger pieces. Omit the cheese from the sauce but add 1 can (6 oz.) sliced mushrooms, drained. Turkey can be used instead of chicken and pie crust, see page 122, if preferred.

   Game pie: Use cooked grouse, pheasant or partridge pieces in the chicken pie, omit the cheese and make the sauce with game stock.

To freeze:
Prepare the pie, freeze, wrap and use within 2–3 months. Thaw out before cooking. If more convenient to cook the pie first, reheat gently from the frozen state.

To economize:
Omit the rather expensive peppers and flavor the sauce with cooked peas and carrots.

Turkey Pudding

To make: 30 minutes   **To cook:** 2–3 hours   **Serves 4–6**

2½ cups cooked diced turkey meat
2 onions
veal stuffing made with 2 cups soft
   breadcrumbs (see page 83)
1–2 tablespoons flour
salt and pepper
suet crust pastry made with 2½ cups
   all-purpose flour, etc. (see page 72)
little turkey stock (see method)

This is an excellent dish to make if you buy part of a turkey; use some for roasting, see page 87 and some in this recipe. Dice the meat and chop the onions. Form the stuffing into 1-inch balls. Coat the meat, onions and the stuffing balls in the flour mixed with salt and pepper. Make the pastry and line the bowl as described under Steak and Kidney Pudding, page 72. Fill with turkey mixture and stuffing balls. Add enough stock to come half way up the mixture. Cover with pastry, seal edges, cover with greased foil and steam for 3 hours, see page 72.

To serve:
With mixed vegetables.

To vary:
Rabbit pudding: As above, but omit the stuffing balls. Mix a little freshly chopped or dried sage with the rabbit, etc. and add diced bacon and diced carrots.

To freeze:
Cook for 2½ hours to make sure the pastry is light. Cool, wrap and freeze. Allow to thaw, then heat for 1 hour. Can also be prepared, but not steamed, then frozen. Use within 2 months.

Chicken pie

Game Turnovers

To make: 30 minutes **To cook:** 50 minutes plus making stock **Serves 4**

2–3 young pigeons, or 1 small young
   pheasant or ½ large young rabbit
2–3 medium-sized onions
4 medium-sized potatoes
3 tablespoons game stock (see
   method)
salt and pepper
pinch fines herbes
pie crust made with 3 cups
   all-purpose flour, etc. (see page
   122)
To glaze:
1 egg

Remove all the raw meat from the bones of the bird or rabbit; simmer the
bones to give stock (any remaining stock can be used in a gravy to serve
with the hot turnovers or in soup). Cut the meat into ¼–½-inch cubes. Peel
the onions and potatoes, cut into the same-sized pieces. Mix with the
stock, salt, pepper and herbs. Roll out the pastry to about ¼-inch
thickness. Cut into 4 large rounds. Put a quarter of the game mixture into
the center of each pastry round. Brush the edges of the pastry with water,
fold over and seal firmly, forming a half-moon shape. Place on a greased
cookie sheet. Brush with beaten egg. Bake for 20–25 minutes in a hot oven,
400–425°F. to brown the pastry, then lower the heat to moderate, 350°F. for
a further 25–30 minutes.
To serve:
Hot or cold with vegetables or salad. Can be served with gravy made by
thickening the leftover game stock with flour.
To vary:
Cornish Turnovers: Use diced beef rump or top round.
To freeze:
Do not freeze uncooked turnovers as the potato will spoil; these are better
eaten freshly made.

Using Cooked Meat & Poultry

I have grouped the recipes for using cooked meat and poultry together in this section as the recipes I have chosen are equally successful with either. You will notice however that I have adapted the herbs and flavoring according to the meat or poultry used. Remember cooked meat or poultry can be rather dry, so give flavor and an interesting texture to the food with good sauces.

Note: When reheating cooked poultry or meat it is essential that this be thoroughly heated and not just warmed for a few minutes. This rule applies also when reheating left-over stews. The liquid must come to a boil and be maintained at this temperature for some minutes.

Ragoût of Duckling

To make: 25 minutes   **To cook:** 1 hour   **Serves 4**

¼ cup fat
2 onions
¼ cup flour
2 cups duck stock or water and 2 chicken bouillon cubes
½–1 teaspoon freshly chopped or pinch dried sage
2 large carrots
1 can (10 oz.) natural whole chestnuts, drained
¼ cup port wine
enough roasted duckling for 4
salt and pepper
To garnish:
1–2 navel oranges

Although this is a good way to use up pieces of cooked duckling, it is also a practical recipe when entertaining, as it can be prepared earlier and heated when required. If roasting duckling for this dish, do not over-cook, and cut into serving-size pieces.

Heat the fat and sauté the chopped onions for 4–5 minutes. Stir in the flour, then stir over low heat for 2–3 minutes. Gradually stir in the stock or water and bouillon cubes. Bring to a boil and cook until thickened. Add the sage and diced carrots. Cover the pan, simmer for 40 minutes, then add the chestnuts, port wine and pieces of duckling. Heat until hot. Season to taste with salt and pepper. Garnish with orange slices.

To serve:
With apple sauce, page 82, and an orange salad, page 110.

To vary:
Use game birds or rabbit, hare, goose, chicken, turkey, sliced cooked meat, cooked chops of pork or lamb.

To freeze:
Cook, cool then freeze and use within 2 months. I prefer to add the chestnuts and port wine when reheating this dish.

Note:
If you like the crisp skin on duckling or goose do not add the poultry to the sauce as described above. Prepare the sauce in the pan, then transfer to a large, heated shallow heatproof dish. Lay the portions of poultry on this, skin side up. Cover the dish and heat thoroughly for about 30 minutes in a moderate oven, 350°F. Remove the lid and place under broiler for a few minutes to crisp skin.

Chicken Cutlets

To make: 25 minutes   **To cook:** 20 minutes   **Serves 4**

1½ cups cooked chicken
2 tablespoons chicken fat or margarine
6 tablespoons flour
⅔ cup chicken stock or milk
1 cup soft breadcrumbs
1 tablespoon chopped parsley
salt and pepper
1 egg
⅔ cup dry breadcrumbs
To fry:
little fat or oil

Grind chicken with a fine blade in grinder. Make a thick sauce with the chicken fat or margarine, 4 tablespoons of the flour and the stock or milk; stir well as the mixture thickens, see page 54. Add the chicken, soft breadcrumbs and parsley and season to taste with salt and pepper and chill. Form into chop shapes, coat in the remaining flour mixed with salt and pepper then in beaten egg and dry breadcrumbs. Fry for about 4–5 minutes on each side in hot shallow fat or oil. Drain on absorbent paper.

To serve:
Hot with vegetables or cold with salad.

To vary:
Use any left-over cooked ground meat or poultry. Vary the binding sauce as required; use a brown stock with meat. A little wine can be added to the sauce, if wished. If you have left-over stuffing, grind or chop this and add to the mixture, in which case use slightly less soft breadcrumbs. Double the amount of fat or margarine and sauté 1–2 finely chopped onions in this, then make the sauce.

Rissoles: These are made in the same way as the cutlets, but the mixture is formed into flat round cakes or patties.

To freeze:
Either cook and freeze, or prepare and freeze. Use within 1 month. Do not wrap the cutlets until frozen hard, otherwise the coating sticks to the wrapping.

Ragoût of duckling

Chicken Suprême

To make: 15 minutes **To cook:** 30–40 minutes **Serves 4**

8 mushrooms
2 sprigs parsley
1 small onion
2 tablespoons butter
¼ cup flour
1¼ cups chicken stock or water and 1
    chicken bouillon cube
2 teaspoons lemon juice
12 oz. cooked chicken slices
1 egg yolk
⅓ cup heavy cream
salt and pepper
For the rice:
1⅓ cups long grain rice
2½ cups water
½–1 teaspoon salt
3 tablespoons chopped parsley
Quick tip:
Use canned mushrooms and instant
minced onions or heat the chicken in
condensed cream of chicken soup.
Flavor with sherry.

Chop the mushrooms, parsley and onion. Melt the butter in a saucepan
and sauté vegetables for 5 minutes. Stir in the flour and cook for 1 minute.
Gradually stir in the stock or water and bouillon cube, bring to a boil,
stirring all the time. Reduce heat, cover the pan and simmer very gently for
20–30 minutes. Strain the sauce if wished and stir in the lemon juice. Slice
the chicken; the skin can be left on for extra flavor and color. Add to the
sauce and heat the chicken through for about 5 minutes. Mix the egg yolk
with the cream, season then stir in ¼ cup of the hot chicken sauce. Stir the
cream mixture into the pan and heat without boiling. Put the rice, water,
salt and parsley into a saucepan. Bring to a boil and stir once. Cover and
simmer for 15 minutes or until the rice is tender and all the liquid is
absorbed.

To serve:
Put the rice around the edge of the serving dish and spoon the chicken and
sauce into the center.
To vary:
Add 1–2½ tablespoons dry sherry to the egg yolk and cream.
To freeze:
This dish can be frozen, but there is a possibility of the sauce curdling. It is
better to make the sauce without the egg yolk and cream. Heat gently
adding the egg yolk and cream just before serving. Use within 2–3 months.
To economize:
If using a smaller amount of poultry, make a more satisfying meal by
topping with sliced hard-cooked egg.
Note: This recipe is an ideal dish for an invalid. It may be a good idea to
omit the mushrooms, parsley and onion and simply to serve the chicken
coated with the plain sauce suprême. To give extra food value make the
sauce with half stock and half milk. Use milk instead of heavy cream.

95

Chicken Pilau

To make: 15 minutes   **To cook:** 35–40 minutes   **Serves 4–5**

2 onions
1 clove garlic (optional)
3 tablespoons chicken fat or oil
1⅓ cups long grain rice
2½ cups chicken stock made by
    simmering the chicken carcass or
    giblets
⅓ cup raisins
few pine or other nuts (optional)
2 cups diced cooked chicken
salt and pepper
To garnish:
few nuts or dry breadcrumbs
Quick tip:
Use instant minced onion and garlic
salt.

Peel and chop the onions, crush the garlic. Sauté in the hot chicken fat or oil for a few minutes, then add the rice stirring until golden. Add the stock, bring to a boil and stir. Simmer in an open pan for about 10 minutes. Add remaining ingredients, then cook for a further 10–15 minutes until the liquid has just been absorbed. Season to taste with salt and pepper. Pile on to a hot dish and top with the nuts or crumbs.

To serve:
With salad or a green vegetable.

To vary:
Use diced cooked turkey or lean lamb instead of chicken. Use uncooked chicken or turkey in the basic recipe. Allow at least 2½ cups boned diced raw chicken or turkey. Fry this in the hot oil with the onions and garlic, then add the rice and proceed as the basic recipe.

Use uncooked, diced lamb in the basic recipe. The ideal cut would be a thick slice, weighing 1¼ lb. from the top of the leg. Dice the lamb and fry with the onions and garlic. Add the rice and proceed as the basic recipe, allow 20 minutes cooking time and increase the amount of liquid slightly.

To freeze:
Do not freeze this dish, but frozen cooked chicken could be used. Thaw sufficiently to dice.

The reason for not recommending freezing is that much of the delicate flavor seems to be lost; lamb pilau is better. If you decide to freeze it use within 1 month. Freeze the mixture lightly, shake the container to break up the rice, then continue freezing.

To economize:
Use only a small quantity of chicken and add left-over cooked vegetables.

Chicken pilau

Buying Delicatessen Cooked Meats & Poultry

The recipes on pages 94–96 and those that follow, could be made with either home-cooked meats and poultry or those you buy ready-cooked. Delicatessen counters in the supermarkets usually provide a wide variety of cooked meats. Most of these can be eaten with salad, and make a very easy meal but some are particularly suitable for using as the basis for hot dishes.

Diced cooked ham, tongue, turkey or chicken can be heated in a white sauce. It improves the flavor of the sauce if you let the meat stand in this for a while or if you add a chicken bouillon cube. Use as a filling for omelets, crêpes or a savory topping on toast.

If preferred the meat or poultry can be chopped very finely and added to the beaten eggs before making an omelet. Salami and garlic sausage can also be used in this way.

A good way to use a little left-over cooked meat or poultry is to dice it, heat it in the margarine or butter used to scramble eggs, then add the beaten eggs and cook in the usual way.

Ham in cherry sauce:
Make half the quantity of cherry sauce as given on page 89, under Caneton aux cerises, but use water and 1 chicken bouillon cube instead of giblet stock. When the sauce has thickened add 4 thick slices boiled ham and heat. Serve with a salad. Serves 4.

Ham in Cumberland sauce:
Mix 1¼ cups water with 2 teaspoons cornstarch. Put into a pan with 1 chicken bouillon cube, the finely grated rind and juice of 2 oranges, 1 teaspoon prepared mustard and ¼ cup redcurrant jelly. Stir over low heat until thickened and clear, then add 4 thick slices boiled ham and heat. This sauce is also excellent with cold ham, but use only half the amount of water, stock and cornstarch, then let the sauce cool. Serves 4.

Tongue in Madeira sauce:
Make a sauce with 2 tablespoons fat or margarine, ¼ cup flour and 1¼ cups beef broth or water and 1 beef bouillon cube, see page 82. Add ⅓ cup Madeira, season with salt and pepper and add 2 tablespoons parsley. When the sauce is really hot, stir in ½ lb. sliced cooked tongue and heat. Serve with diced carrots. Serves 4.

Turkey & Ham Medallions

For the puff pastry:
2 cups all-purpose flour
pinch salt
juice of ½ a lemon
water to mix (see method)
1 cup (2 sticks) slightly softened
  butter, preferably unsalted
For the topping:
1⅓ cups chopped cooked turkey
1⅓ cups chopped cooked ham
¼ cup butter or turkey fat
½ cup flour
2 cups turkey stock or water and 2
  chicken bouillon cubes or half stock
  and half milk
salt and pepper
Quick tip:
Use 1 lb. frozen puff pastry.

To make: 40 minutes plus standing   **To bake:** 15 minutes   **Makes about 20**

Sift the flour with the salt, add the lemon juice and enough cold water to make a stiff dough. Knead until an elastic dough that is easily rolled out. Roll to an oblong shape 10 × 12 inches. Shape butter into a flat cake and place in the center of the oblong. Bring up the bottom one-third of the dough (the 10-inch side) and fold over the butter. Bring down the top one-third until the butter is completely covered. It is rather like an open, then a closed envelope. Turn the pastry at right angles, seal the ends then "rib" the pastry (this means depress it at regular intervals). Roll out again lightly but firmly, do not exert undue pressure at this stage, until an oblong shape again. Bring up the bottom third and bring down the top third again. Turn the pastry at right angles, seal the ends, "rib" the pastry, chill 20 minutes. Continue as before. Altogether the pastry must have 7 foldings and 7 rollings before it is ready to use. Leave to rest for about 30 minutes before using. Roll out very thinly, cut into rounds, fingers or diamond shapes or other desired shapes. Put on an ungreased shallow baking pan and bake for 10–15 minutes in a very hot oven, 475°F. Lower the heat after 5–8 minutes. Mince the turkey and ham and make a fairly thick sauce with the butter or turkey fat, flour and stock, see page 54. Add the meat and season with salt and pepper.
To serve:
Top puff pastry medallions with the turkey and ham mixture and serve hot. Serve with vegetables or salad.

Shepherd's Pie

To make: 25 minutes   **To cook:** 55 minutes   **Serves 4**

1½ lbs. potatoes
salt and pepper
6 tablespoons margarine
3–4 tablespoons milk
12 oz. chopped cooked meat or
  poultry
1–2 onions
2–3 tomatoes
1 tablespoon flour
1–1¼ cups stock or water and 1 beef or
  chicken bouillon cube
pinch fines herbes
Quick tip:
Use canned stew. Add fried onions to
this and top with reconstituted
seasoned instant mashed potatoes.

Peel the potatoes, cook in boiling salted water until tender, then drain and mash with 2 tablespoons of the margarine and the milk, season with salt and pepper. Grind or dice the meat or poultry, peel and chop the onions, skin and chop the tomatoes and sauté the onions and tomatoes in 3 tablespoons of the margarine for about 8–10 minutes; take care the onions do not brown. Stir in the flour then gradually stir in stock or water and bouillon cube. Stir in the meat or poultry, herbs and seasoning. Put into a pie plate or casserole. Top with the mashed potato and drizzle with remaining melted margarine. Bake for about 25–30 minutes in a moderate oven, 375°F.
To serve:
Hot with green or mixed vegetables.
To vary:
Top the meat or poultry mixture with halved or thickly sliced hard-cooked eggs.
   Flavor the meat or poultry mixture with a little curry powder.
To freeze:
This freezes well; do not add eggs. Use within 6 weeks.

Beef Fritters

To make: 10 minutes   **To cook:** 3–6 minutes   **Serves 4–6**

batter made with 1 cup all-purpose
  flour, etc. (see coating fish, page 44)
12 oz. cooked corned beef
To fry:
deep fat or oil

Make the batter as page 44, but for a very light result use self-rising flour or all-purpose flour with 1 teaspoon baking powder. Cut the corned beef into thin slices, or, if it shows signs of breaking, dice it. Coat the slices with the batter or mix the diced beef into the batter. Fry for about 3 minutes until golden brown, see page 44. Diced beef in batter should be spooned into hot fat. Drain on absorbent paper.
To serve:
Hot as a light snack or main dish.
To freeze:
Do not freeze.

Savory Meat Slice

To make: 20 minutes   **To cook:** 45–50 minutes   **Serves 4**

1 large onion
2 large tomatoes
2 tablespoons drippings or fat
1⅓ cups chopped cooked meat,
  chicken or corned beef
pinch fines herbes
salt and pepper
suet crust pastry made with 2 cups
  all-purpose flour (see page 72)
To glaze:
1 egg or a little milk

Peel and chop the onion and skin and chop the tomatoes. Sauté in the hot drippings or fat. Stir in ground meat, herbs and salt and pepper. Allow to cool. Roll out the suet crust pastry until just over ¼-inch thickness, cut into two oblongs. Lift one oblong on to a greased cookie sheet. Cover with the filling, then the second oblong of pastry. Seal the edges with the tines of a fork, score the top lightly into diamonds and brush with beaten egg or milk. Bake for approximately 35–40 minutes in a hot oven, 425–450°F., lowering the heat to 400°F. after 20 minutes.
To serve:
Hot with mixed vegetables.
To freeze:
This is better eaten fresh, or prepared but not cooked and frozen. Use within 1 month.

Speedy Chicken Curry

To make: 10 minutes   **No cooking**   **Serves 4**

8 slices cooked chicken
1¼ cups plain yogurt
½–1 tablespoon curry powder
1 tablespoon tomato ketchup
salt and pepper
few green onions
1–2 tablespoons raisins

Remove skin from slices of chicken, so they absorb the dressing more readily. Mix the yogurt, curry powder, tomato ketchup, chopped green onions (use grated onion when these are not available) and raisins. Season to taste with salt and pepper. Put the chicken in a dish, pour over the dressing and leave for a short time.
To serve:
In a border of the Rice and Vegetable salad, see page 107.
To freeze:
Do not freeze this dish, but thawed frozen cooked chicken could be used.

Toad in the Hole

Make a batter with 1 cup all-purpose flour, pinch salt, 2 eggs, 1¼ cups milk and 1 tablespoon oil or melted butter, see page 137. Heat 2 tablespoons fat in a shallow casserole, then add 1 lb. sausages. Bake for about 10 minutes in a hot oven, 425°F. Pour in the batter and return to a very hot oven 425°–450°F. for about 25–30 minutes. If using a 450°F. oven, which is ideal to give a light batter, lower the heat slightly after 10–15 minutes so the batter does not get too brown before it is baked. Serve with vegetables.

To vary:
Instead of sausages you can use canned cocktail frankfurters as in the picture, lambs kidneys, tomatoes, mushrooms, fingers of cooked steak or roast beef or a selection of these.

To freeze:
Do not freeze this dish, but frozen sausages could be used.

Sweet & Sour Medley

To make: 20 minutes **To cook:** 20 minutes **Serves 6–8**

For the sauce:
2 large cooking apples
2–3 tablespoons honey or brown
 sugar
1 tablespoon cornstarch
⅔ cup beef stock or water and ½ beef
 bouillon cube
1 tablespoon vinegar
3 tablespoons mustard pickle
For the medley:
1⅓ cups diced cooked chicken
⅔ cup diced cooked ham
1⅓ cups diced cooked beef
1⅓ cups diced cooked pork
1 small cauliflower
3–4 medium-sized onions
little milk
little cornstarch (see method)
To fry:
little oil or fat

Peel, core and slice the apples, simmer with the honey or sugar until soft, then beat hard or sieve or whirl in a blender for a very smooth mixture. Blend the cornstarch with the stock, or water and bouillon cube. Add this to the apple purée, stir over low heat until thickened and smooth. Add the vinegar and chopped pickle; keep hot while cooking the meat and vegetables. Cut the cauliflower into small flowerets, there is no need to pre-cook these as they are very good as a crisp contrast to the meat but if you like you can boil them for 2–3 minutes only. Peel the onions, cut into slices then separate into rings. Dip the chicken, meat and vegetables into milk, then coat in cornstarch. Fry in the hot oil or fat, 1 inch deep for 2–3 minutes only. When using raw chicken or steak lower the heat and cook more slowly for a few more minutes. Drain on absorbent paper.

To serve:
Arrange the fried meat and vegetables on a large hot dish, spear on toothpicks. Place the bowl of hot sauce in the center. This can also be served for a main dish with rice or crispy fried noodles, see page 131.

To freeze:
Although thawed chicken and meat could be diced and used, the fried meat and vegetables must be served freshly cooked. The sauce can be frozen, but tends to lose flavor.

Vegetables and Salads

We are very fortunate in having a good selection of fresh, frozen, canned and dried vegetables from which to choose. Serve vegetables often, for they are an important food as they supply many of the minerals, vitamins and roughage we need for good health.

Shop wisely for fresh vegetables; good markets have daily deliveries, so they are in prime condition when you buy them. Store root vegetables in a cool, airy place and put other vegetables into a covered container in the refrigerator.

To cook vegetables: Follow the directions on packages or cans and do not over-cook. Prepare fresh vegetables just before cooking, if possible, as long soaking destroys some of their food value; this applies particularly to green vegetables. If boiling put into boiling salted water; the old adage used to be "anything that grows above the ground goes into boiling water, anything that grows below the ground goes into cold water." We have now learned that all vegetables are better placed into boiling water if we are to retain maximum flavor, color and vitamins. Serve as soon as possible after cooking.

Economical vegetable dishes: Treat vegetables as a dish in themselves, as well as an accompaniment to meat, fish, etc. Platters of mixed cooked vegetables can be served with a cheese sauce. If you include cooked peas, beans and/or lentils you will have more than an adequate amount of protein for the family's needs.

Cooked vegetables can be used as a filling in crêpes, omelets (see the Spanish-type omelet on page 126) or can be added to a batter to make a vegetable "Toad in the Hole" as page 99.

To freeze: You will find information on freezing foods throughout this book and also on page 10. If you grow, or can obtain stocks of really fresh young vegetables, it is worth freezing these yourself. However, if you cannot, then I would suggest you are better to buy commercially frozen ones. Firms which freeze vegetables have become experts at knowing which varieties to freeze, and they also pick and freeze the vegetables within a matter of hours, so the young fresh taste is retained.

If you do freeze your own vegetables, you will find detailed instructions in freezer books. Here, however, are the basic steps you need to take, after selecting the right vegetables.

a) Prepare the vegetables as for cooking.

b) "Blanch" them as shown in the picture. This means immersing in boiling water for a recommended time, to destroy harmful enzymes that might be present and so retain the color, texture and flavor. It is important to follow instructions on "blanching" time and the quantity of vegetables to handle at one time.

c) Cool rapidly, to prevent over-softening in ice water.

d) Pack carefully to exclude the air, seal and freeze.

e) Place close to freezer coils for rapid freezing the first 12 hours.

f) If freezing dry-pack, freeze vegetables in a single layer on cookie sheets. Pour when hard, into freezer containers.

g) Label so you know what is in the package.

Frozen vegetables can be stored for 1 year.

It is also worthwhile freezing small containers of cooked vegetables to use in salads, see page 107 and omelets, see page 126. Do not over-cook these so they retain the maximum flavor and use within 3–4 months.

Note: Some vegetables cannot be frozen, see page 10. The keeping times for cooked vegetable dishes will vary according to the particular recipe, and these are given in this section.

Vegetable risotto

Vegetable Risotto

To make: 25 minutes   **To cook:** 30 minutes   **Serves 4–6**

2 large onions
2 cloves garlic (optional)
3 tablespoons oil
1 lb. tomatoes
1 cup long grain rice
2½ cups water
2–3 large carrots
¾ cup peas (fresh, frozen or canned)
salt and pepper
1 cup sliced mushrooms
3–4 tablespoons chopped parsley
2 cups (8 oz.) grated Gruyère or
   Cheddar cheese

Quick tip:
Choose canned peas, canned
tomatoes (use liquid from can in place
of some of the water), canned
mushrooms and instant minced
onions.

Slice the peeled onions, separate into rings and crush the cloves of garlic, if used. Sauté for a few minutes in the hot oil, then remove some of the onion rings. Skin and slice the tomatoes. Stir a few slices into the onion mixture, together with the rice, mix thoroughly. Add the water, bring to a boil. Finely dice or coarsely grate the scraped carrots and add to the pan with the peas, if fresh or frozen. Cook for about 10 minutes until the rice and vegetables are beginning to become more tender, season with salt and pepper. Slice the mushrooms and add with the remaining tomato slices and onion rings and canned peas, if using these. Cook gently, stirring a few times until the rice is tender and most of the liquid is absorbed. Stir in half the parsley and half the cheese. Pile on a hot dish, top with remaining parsley and cheese.

To serve:
As a light supper dish with a salad.

To vary:
Add pieces of diced cooked chicken or meat during cooking; it is then important to use within 2–3 months if freezing the risotto.

To freeze:
Rice does lose some texture when frozen but if you want to prepare in advance or freeze any left-over, cook then cool. Pack into a container, freeze lightly, then break up by handling the container and continue freezing or freeze by dry-pack method (page 100). Use within 4–5 months.

To economize:
This is an inexpensive recipe but use left-over pieces of hard cheese.

Some Basic Ways to Cook Vegetables

To bake:
Certain vegetables are delicious baked in the oven, the most usual, and popular, being potatoes. Scrub the potatoes; if you want a really crisp skin rub this with melted fat, margarine or oil. A medium to large-size potato, in a moderately hot oven, 375–400°F. bakes in about 1 hour, but can be baked for a longer period at a lower temperature. It is not advisable to bake it any quicker. Cut a cross in the top of the cooked potato, put a piece of butter, cream cheese, cottage cheese, sour cream mixed with chopped parsley or chives on top, then serve.

When the potato is baked it can be filled in many ways. Halve the potato, scoop out the pulp, mash with salt and pepper and butter, then add:
a) Grated Parmesan cheese
b) Crumbled crisp bacon and chopped tomatoes
c) Cooked sliced mushrooms
d) Beaten egg and Cheddar cheese
e) Cubes of blue cheese, a little plain yogurt and chopped parsley. Top with a slice of crisp bacon and garnish with parsley.
Return the pulp to the potato skin and heat again in the oven.

Onions are also delicious baked. Peel the onions and bake at 350°F. in a little butter and milk, basting once or twice during cooking until onions are easily pierced but still hold their shape.

To boil:
The most usual way to cook vegetables is by boiling and this is introduced on page 100. The vegetables are put into boiling salted water, using just the minimum amount, then cooked quickly in a covered pan for the shortest possible time. One exception to the rule of quick cooking is potatoes. If you boil these too quickly they become broken on the outside, before they are cooked in the center, so cook these slowly and gently. Drain the vegetables, add margarine or butter and chopped parsley or chives, and toss to coat all pieces, then serve or use in the recipes on page 107. In order to shorten the cooking time it is a good idea to shred green vegetables finely just before cooking, and to break cauliflower or broccoli into flowerets.

Carrots and other root vegetables are delicious if cooked in a good white or brown stock. Use the minimum amount and lift the lid as the vegetables come to the end of the cooking time, so excess liquid evaporates, top with chopped parsley. Shredded green cabbage and Brussels sprouts can be cooked in tomato juice or a mixture of tomato juice and water or chicken stock. Strain the cooked vegetables and thicken remaining liquid with a little flour or cornstarch, serve as a sauce over the vegetables.

To braise:
This is an interesting way of cooking onions, leeks and quartered hearts of celery. Prepare the vegetables, then sauté in a little hot margarine, butter or drippings. Remove from the pan, make a brown sauce, see page 82 and when this has thickened replace the vegetables in the sauce, cover the pan and simmer steadily until tender. Serve in the sauce.

To broil:
Tomatoes and mushrooms can be cooked under the broiler and this is a particularly good way of cooking, when fish, meat or poultry are being broiled. Prepare the vegetables and brush with plenty of butter seasoned with salt and pepper. Either put on the broiler pan itself, heat for 1–2 minutes then put the rest of the food on the pan and continue cooking together or, if preferred, start to cook the meat or fish then add the vegetables towards the end of the cooking time.

Vegetables can be put on skewers, as in the Herbed Kebabs on page 66, or mixed with diced cheese.

To fry vegetables:
Not all vegetables are suitable for frying; the best vegetables to use are eggplants, zucchini, mushrooms, onions, potatoes, green tomatoes.

To fry eggplants and zucchini:
Slice, coat in flour mixed with salt and pepper or egg and crumbs or batter, see page 44, then fry in shallow or deep fat until brown on both sides.

To fry onions:
Cut into rings, coat with flour mixed with salt and pepper, or milk and flour, or batter, see page 44 and fry in shallow or deep oil as above.

To fry tomatoes and mushrooms:
Fry in a little shallow fat or margarine for a few minutes.

To fry potatoes:
Cut the potatoes into the desired shape, i.e. fingers, slices, strips. Dry well. To shallow fry, heat enough oil or fat to give a ½-inch depth in the pan. Fry potatoes until golden brown and crisp, turn once; or fry twice, as for deep frying below.

To deep fry:
Half fill a pan with oil or use enough fat to half fill the pan when melted. Do not over-fill. Heat the frying basket in the pan, so the potatoes will not stick to this. Test the oil or fat before adding the potatoes; at the right temperature, a cube of day-old bread should turn golden brown within 1 minute (it is a little quicker with oil than fat). Put some of the potatoes into the frying basket, do not over-fill. Fry at 360°F. until soft, remove from the pan and drain. Fry the next batch in the same way. Before serving, reheat the oil or fat and fry the potatoes quickly for 2 minutes until crisp and brown. Drain on absorbent paper. Frozen French fries only need one frying.

To roast vegetables:
Potatoes, parsnips and onions are the most popular vegetables to roast. Peel the vegetables, cut potatoes and parsnips into halves or quarters, depending on size and leave onions whole. Parsnips do not roast well unless they are first boiled for 15–20 minutes in boiling salted water. Opinions vary about the advisability of par-boiling potatoes for part of the cooking time. If you like them to be "mealy" in the center then boil slowly for 10–15 minutes, depending upon the size, then drain. Dry the raw or cooked vegetables well, then stir into very hot fat in the roasting pan, so they are evenly coated. Cook parsnips and raw potatoes for about 1 hour, par-boiled potatoes for about 45 minutes and medium-sized onions for 1–1¼ hours in a moderately hot to hot oven, 400–425°F.

Zucchini à la Grecque

1 lb. small zucchini
salt and pepper
⅓ cup olive oil
juice of 1 lemon
1¼ cups water
1 bay leaf
¼–½ teaspoon chopped lemon thyme or ¼ teaspoon dried thyme
6 crushed peppercorns
¼ teaspoon coriander seeds
2 large tomatoes
1 clove garlic
Quick tip:
Use well drained canned tomatoes and garlic salt.

To make: 15 minutes plus standing   **To cook:** 30 minutes   **Serves 4–6**

Wash and dry the zucchini and cut off ends and any damaged skin. Cut into ½–1-inch slices. Spread on a flat dish and sprinkle very lightly with salt, leave for 30–45 minutes; this extracts the surplus liquid which should be poured away. This stage is not essential but saves having to drain off liquid later. If more convenient, stand in a colander and leave for 1 hour, then drain well. Bring the oil, lemon juice, water, bay leaf, thyme, peppercorns and coriander seeds to a boil in a saucepan. Add the skinned and chopped tomatoes and well drained and dried zucchini. Cook quickly for 20 minutes in an uncovered saucepan. Drain off any excess water if necessary. Add the crushed garlic, salt and pepper and chill before serving.

To serve:
As a vegetable hors d'oeuvre or with a main dish.

To vary:
Mix sliced green and red peppers with the zucchini.

To freeze:
This freezes excellently. Use within 8–9 months.

To economize:
Use unpeeled diced summer squash.

Zucchini à la grecque

Some Ways to Serve Vegetables

You will find some ideas for vegetable dishes in the pages that follow, but here are some very quick and easy ways of turning cooked vegetables into interesting dishes.

Vegetables mornay:
Make a cheese sauce as the recipe on page 54 while the vegetables are cooking. You can make the sauce with all milk, but I find the flavor is better if I use just a little of the vegetable water (which contains a great deal of flavor as well as minerals and vitamins) and a little less milk. Drain the vegetables, pour the sauce over and garnish with chopped parsley, sliced tomatoes or chopped chives.

Vegetable crêpes:
Make crêpes, see page 137. Cook vegetables and mix with white, cheese or parsley sauce, pages 54 and 82. Fill cooked crêpes with vegetable mixture and serve. A more interesting dish is made by topping the filled crêpes with extra sauce and browning this lightly under the broiler.

Vegetable pie:
Prepare the vegetables and put into a pie dish. Cover with a white, cheese or parsley sauce, pages 54 and 82, then with creamy mashed potatoes. Bake in the oven at 400°F. until crisp and brown, or, if all the ingredients are hot, brown under the broiler.

Vegetables niçoise:
Make a good tomato sauce, see below, and mix the vegetables with this; serve topped with grated cheese.

To make a tomato sauce:
Heat 2 tablespoons margarine in a pan and gently sauté a chopped onion, a chopped slice of bacon (optional) and a crushed clove garlic (optional) for 2–3 minutes. Add 1 lb. skinned chopped tomatoes, ⅔ cup water, salt and pepper and a good pinch sugar. Simmer gently in a covered pan for 15 minutes, then sieve or blend and use.
See also vegetable soufflé, page 121 and Spanish omelet, page 126.

Rice and vegetable salad:
Although left-over vegetables can be used for this salad, it is nicer if you cook them fresh and mix them with hot cooked rice. It can be served hot instead of the risotto on page 102, or mix with mayonnaise, see page 111 and chopped herbs and allow to cool. This is excellent with fish.

Sweetcorn Scallops

To make: 20 minutes   **To bake:** 30 minutes   **Serves 6**

1 package (10 oz.) frozen kernel corn
2 cups white sauce (see page 55)
3 tablespoons heavy cream
pinch cayenne pepper
pinch ground nutmeg
salt and pepper
2 tablespoons butter
⅔ cup dry breadcrumbs
To garnish:
6 slices thick-sliced bacon
parsley sprigs
Quick tip:
Use canned sweetcorn, drain and use the liquid in the white sauce.

Cook the corn according to the directions on the package, drain well. Make the white sauce as page 54, then add the cream, cayenne pepper, nutmeg and salt and pepper to taste. Stir in the corn and divide between 6 scallop dishes or shells. Heat the butter in a shallow frying pan, then stir in breadcrumbs. Sprinkle over the scallops. Place on a cookie sheet and bake in a moderate oven, 350–375°F. for 15–30 minutes or until heated through. Roll up each bacon slice tightly and thread on a metal skewer. Either cook the bacon rolls in the oven with the scallops or under a broiler (turning occasionally if using the broiler) until cooked and crisp.
To serve:
Place the scallops on small plates and garnish with the bacon rolls and parsley sprigs.
To freeze:
Do not freeze this dish.
To economize:
Use left-over diced cooked vegetables in place of sweetcorn.

Preparing Salads

A salad depends not only upon using really fresh ingredients, but in preparing and serving these well.

Green salad vegetables should be washed thoroughly, but carefully in cold water, then shaken dry in a salad basket or drained on cloth or paper towels. Do this very carefully, otherwise you can bruise the delicate leaves, this is particularly important with Boston or field lettuce. Tomatoes that are ripe can be skinned if desired, just lower into boiling water, leave for 30 seconds, lift out, then lower into cold water. This prevents the tomato becoming too soft. The skin comes away immediately.

Red and green peppers can be diced or cut into rings. Discard the seeds. If you like pepper flesh slightly soft, "blanch" by putting into boiling salted water and heating for a few minutes, drain and use.

Radishes should be washed, then sliced or served whole or cut into fancy shapes.

Cucumber can be peeled or the peel can be left on. To give a serrated edge run the tines of a fork down the skin of the cucumber, then slice.

Apples can be added to salads; remember the flesh discolours, so dip in lemon juice or coat in mayonnaise. Most other fruits blend well in a salad, they add flavor and colour, see page 110.

Simple salads

Use these salads as the basis for other more imaginative ideas.

Green salad:
This blends with most ingredients and is the salad generally served with hot, as well as cold dishes. Choose lettuce or other greens, wash as above, dry, then shred — it is better not to cut lettuce, but to shred it with your fingers. Mix with watercress, diced green pepper, sliced or diced cucumber, celery or chicory, but do not add tomatoes or hard-cooked eggs. Toss with French dressing, see page 110, just before serving and top with chopped parsley or other green herbs.

Mixed salad:
This term covers almost every selection of salad ingredients, but generally does not mean you have a protein food among the ingredients. It is usually served with meat and fish.

Main dish salads:
These are outlined in the pages that follow, but can be very simple as the anchovy and egg salad picture opposite shows. Simply serve wedges of crisp Iceberg lettuce with hard-cooked eggs, anchovy fillets and other salad ingredients and add dressing to taste, see page 110 and 111.

Ratatouille

To make: 20 minutes   **To cook:** 40–50 minutes   **Serves 4–6**

2 onions
1 lb. tomatoes
1 lb. zucchini
4 very small eggplants
salt and pepper
1 red or green pepper
1–2 cloves garlic
¼ cup oil
To garnish:
1–2 tablespoons chopped parsley
Quick tip:
Use canned tomatoes, but not all the liquid from the can, and instant minced onion.

Chop the peeled onions. Skin the tomatoes and halve or quarter. Slice unpeeled zucchini, discarding just the hard ends. Remove the stalks from the eggplants and dice. If you dislike the rather bitter taste of the skin, score the eggplants with a knife, sprinkle lightly with salt and leave for 15 minutes then cut into pieces. Slice the pepper (discard seeds) and crush the garlic. Heat the oil in a frying pan and gently sauté the onions and garlic. Add the eggplant, zucchini, tomatoes and pepper. Season well with salt and pepper and simmer slowly with a tight lid on the pan, until the vegetables are tender. Stir once or twice during cooking.
To serve:
Hot or cold, sprinkled with parsley. This makes an excellent hors d'oeuvre.
To vary:
Add sliced mushrooms.
To freeze:
Excellent when frozen; use within 1 year.
To economize:
Make the dish when the vegetables are at their cheapest, then freeze.

Anchovy and egg salad

Fruits in Salads

Add seasonal fruits to salads, as most fruits blend well with the vegetables and other ingredients and they add color as well as a refreshing flavor. Soft berry fruits are particularly good with cottage or cream cheese salads as are apples and pears. These also blend with ham, pork or fish salads, but remember the flesh discolors, so dip in lemon juice or coat in mayonnaise to prevent this. Cooked dried fruits, such as apricots and prunes are excellent with cold meat salads.

Orange salad:
This is one of the best accompaniments to roast duckling or goose. Slice skin and white membrane from navel oranges. Cut into sections. Remove seeds and mix orange sections with a green salad and French dressing.

A salad dressing provides both a moist texture and additional flavor to a salad. The two classic dressings, i.e., mayonnaise and French or vinaigrette dressing are given here together with other suggestions.

Avocado dressing:
Halve a ripe avocado as described in the recipe below. Remove seed and skin. Mash the pulp with at least 1 tablespoon lemon juice, then add salt, pepper, a little olive oil and enough plain yogurt or sour cream to give the consistency of a mayonnaise. Flavor with a few drops Worcestershire sauce or extra lemon juice. This is good with chicken or cheese salads.

Blue cheese dressing:
Mash blue cheese with a little oil, lemon juice or vinegar, then add mayonnaise, sour cream or light cream to make a soft consistency.

French or vinaigrette dressing:
Most people like twice the amount of oil to vinegar (wine vinegar is ideal) or lemon juice. Mix the oil into a little prepared mustard then add the lemon juice or vinegar or a mixture of vinegar and lemon juice. Season to taste with salt and pepper. Crushed garlic, a little sugar and chopped fresh herbs can be added for extra flavor. This dressing is used over most salads. Beat again before adding to salad.

Hard-cooked egg mayonnaise:
Press the yolks of 2 hard-cooked eggs through a sieve or mash with a fork, then beat in a little oil, lemon juice and sour cream or extra oil to give the consistency of a thick mayonnaise. Season to taste with salt and pepper. Fresh whipped cream can be added for a richer flavor.

Slimmer's dressing:
Either use lemon or tomato juice on salads or season plain yogurt and flavor with herbs.

Walnut & Avocado Salad

To make: 15 minutes   **No cooking**   **Serves 4**

1–2 tablespoons lemon juice
2 ripe avocados
2 crisp, sweet apples
1/3 cup walnuts
1/4–1/3 cup French dressing (see above)
1 clove garlic (optional)
salt and pepper
To garnish:
few lettuce leaves
Quick tip:
Make a larger supply of French dressing and store in a screw-topped jar. Shake before serving.

Put the lemon juice into a bowl. Cut the avocados carefully in half and remove the seeds. Scrape the pulp gently into the bowl without damaging the skins. Reserve skins. Mash with the lemon juice; this stops it from turning brown. Peel and core the apples, finely chop them and the walnuts and mix with the avocado pulp, the French dressing, crushed garlic, if wished and a little salt and pepper. Mix well and refill the avocado skins. Garnish with lettuce leaves.
To serve:
With thin slices of wholewheat bread and butter.
To vary:
Instead of serving the avocado skins, pile the mixture on a bed of crisp lettuce and surround with sliced cucumber, strips of green pepper and celery sticks. Garnish with extra pieces of walnut or chopped hard-cooked eggs.
To freeze:
Do not freeze this dish. Frozen avocados can be used, see page 12.
To economize:
Use peanuts instead of the more expensive walnuts.

Mayonnaise

2 egg yolks (or you can use whole eggs when making this in a blender, see method)

½–1 teaspoon French or English mustard

salt

pepper (this can include a little paprika)

pinch sugar

1¼ cups olive or other salad oil

1–2½ tablespoons vinegar or lemon juice

1–2½ tablespoons boiling water (optional)

Quick tip:
Use the blender method or an electric mixer to make it.

If making with a blender, use the same recipe, but, because of the speed of blending, you can use whole eggs which give a very light almost "fluffy" mayonnaise. Put the eggs or yolks, salt, pepper, sugar and vinegar or lemon juice into the blender. Switch on for a few seconds, then add the oil gradually, but not drop by drop, through the hole left by removing the cap in the lid or make a foil cover with a hole in the center or a foil funnel, see page 11. Lastly blend in the boiling water.

If making by hand or with a mixer, put the egg yolks only into a clean dry bowl. Add the mustard, salt, pepper and sugar, then add ⅔ cup of the oil, gradually, drop by drop, beating as you do so. If the oil is added too quickly the mayonnaise could curdle. If by any chance this should happen, put another egg yolk into a second bowl and gradually beat in the curdled mayonnaise. When the first half of the oil is blended in you can increase the speed with which you add the rest. There is no need to add the whole cup, but the more oil used the thicker and richer the dressing. Finally beat in 1–2½ tablespoons vinegar (distilled white or white wine vinegar is ideal) or lemon juice. I also like to beat in 1–2½ tablespoons boiling water.

To vary:
Tartar sauce: Add chopped gherkins, chopped parsley and capers to the mayonnaise. Serve with fish salads and hot fish dishes.

Marie Rose dressing: Add tomato paste or ketchup to taste and a little whipped cream and dry sherry with a few drops Worcestershire sauce.

Piquant dressing: This is rather like Tartar sauce but also add a little chopped dill pickle, chopped pimiento and crushed garlic.

To freeze:
Mayonnaise is one of the foods that does not freeze well. If you are likely to waste food blended with mayonnaise, freeze for a short time only.

To economize:
Use only ⅔ cup oil with the egg yolks.

Walnut and avocado salad

Vegetables in Salads

Most left-over cooked vegetables can be added to salads, mixed with mayonnaise and chopped herbs. Grated raw vegetables add a crisp texture as well as being extremely colorful and good to eat; try grated carrot, green or red cabbage (see below), finely shredded raw leek, as well as the more familiar salad vegetables.

One of the most popular vegetable salads is Coleslaw: Ideally this should be made with a green cabbage or even raw Brussels sprouts. Wash, dry and shred the cabbage finely and mix with mayonnaise. This is the basic recipe, only you can add grated carrot, chopped celery or diced apple, chopped nuts, raisins or other dried fruit, chopped gherkins or shredded cucumber.

A tomato and green pepper salad is very good. Cut slices of tomatoes and rings of peppers (discard seeds), arrange on a flat dish and top with French dressing, chopped parsley and chives.

Mix slices of raw red onion and fresh orange sections and top with French dressing.

While left-over cooked potatoes can be used in a potato salad, the flavor is 100% better if freshly cooked, diced, hot potatoes are blended with grated onion or chopped chives and the mayonnaise or French dressing. Allow to cool.

Mushrooms Vinaigrette

To make: 10 minutes   **No cooking**   **Serves 4**

4 oz. fresh mushrooms
¼ cup olive oil
1 tablespoon lemon juice
1 clove garlic
salt and pepper
1 teaspoon finely chopped parsley
Quick tip:
Use well drained canned mushrooms and garlic salt.

Wipe the mushrooms with a clean, damp cloth and leave whole or slice thinly; do not remove the stalks or peel. Combine the oil, lemon juice, crushed garlic, salt, pepper and parsley. Pour the dressing over the mushrooms and make sure they are coated on all sides. Chill, covered for several hours before serving. The raw mushrooms are extremely absorbent so you may have to pour over more of the dressing.
To serve:
Chilled as part of an hors d'oeuvre or with cold meat.
To vary:
Blend 3 tablespoons Vinaigrette dressing (see page 110) with 3 tablespoons mayonnaise and coat the mushrooms.
To freeze:
Do not freeze this dish, although frozen mushrooms could be used.
To economize:
Use less expensive salad oil and vinegar for the dressing.

Mushrooms vinaigrette

112

Main Dish Salads

If you plan a salad for a main course make certain it has plenty of protein, as well as the salad ingredients, so it is satisfying as well as being pleasant to eat.

Most cheese can be served in a salad, either grated, sliced or spooned on a bed of lettuce, etc., as in the case of cottage or cream cheese. Fruit and nuts blend well with all kinds of cheese and children will enjoy this mixture, see the recipe on page 114.

If you are tired of hard-cooked eggs in a salad try rather soft scrambled eggs. Cook the eggs in the usual way, adding chopped parsley and/or chives, then mix in a little mayonnaise as the mixture cools. In Spain the tortilla (Spanish omelet, page 126) is often eaten cold and this is very good with a mixed salad.

White fish may not appear as colorful as shell or oily fish in a salad, but the recipes on page 114 give two ways of making white fish look, as well as taste, interesting.

All salads should be kept covered until ready to serve, but be particularly careful that sliced meat is covered, as it has a tendency to dry, which spoils both the flavor and appearance. The beef and tomato mold, below, is a very simple way of using part of a cooked roast in an economical way, and gives a pleasantly moist texture to the cooked beef.

Beef & Tomato Mold

To make: 15 minutes   **To cook:** 10 minutes   **Serves 4–6**

2 eggs
2½ cups tomato juice
1 envelope unflavored gelatin
1 lb. cooked corned beef
½–1 teaspoon prepared mustard
salt and pepper
To garnish:
lettuce
tomatoes
cucumber

Hard-cook the eggs, crack the shells and plunge into cold water. Remove the shells, but do not chop the eggs until later, as they would become dry. Mix ½ cup tomato juice and gelatin in a pan. Stir over low heat until gelatin is dissolved. Allow this to cool and chill until syrupy. Meanwhile grind or chop the meat very finely and chop the hard-cooked eggs. Stir into the tomato mixture, then add mustard and salt and pepper to taste. Spoon into an oiled 1 quart bowl and chill until firm.
To serve:
Wrap a warm cloth around the mold or bowl or dip into lukewarm water and leave for a few seconds, then invert the mold on a damp serving dish (this enables you to slide it into position if it is not in the center of the dish). Garnish with lettuce, tomatoes and sliced cucumber.
To vary:
Use good stock instead of tomato juice or other meat or poultry; or use half tomato juice and half stock.
To freeze:
Do not freeze this but defrosted cooked meat could be used.
To economize:
Chop other left-over meat or poultry and use instead of beef (see To vary).

Stuffed Eggs

To make: 10 minutes   **To cook:** 10 minutes   **Serves 4–6**

6 eggs
little mayonnaise or softened butter
sardines, ham, anchovy fillets,
    chicken or shrimp (see method)
salt and pepper
To garnish:
lettuce
tomatoes
cucumber

Hard-cook the eggs, crack the shells and plunge into cold water. Remove the shells and allow the eggs to cool slightly. Halve each egg lengthwise, removing the yolks and blend with a little mayonnaise or butter. You can then choose which flavoring you wish, mashed sardines, finely chopped ham, chopped anchovy fillets, ground or diced cooked chicken, chopped shrimp, etc. Taste the mixture, add salt and pepper to taste and spoon the yolks back into the egg whites.
To serve:
On a bed of lettuce, garnished with tomatoes and cucumber. This is good either as a main dish or hors d'oeuvre.
To freeze:
Hard-cooked eggs do not freeze.
To economize:
An ideal way of using small amounts of left-over food.

Fish Cream

To make: 25 minutes plus setting   **To cook:** 10 minutes   **Serves 4**

1 lb. white fish fillets (cod, flounder,
    sole, turbot, haddock)
1¼ cups water
salt and pepper
1 bay leaf
1 envelope unflavored gelatin
3 tablespoons dry sherry
¼ cup mayonnaise
⅔ cup heavy cream
2 teaspoons chopped parsley
Quick tip:
Use canned salmon or tuna, measure
liquid from can and add water to
make up to 1¼ cups.

Put the fish into cold water with salt and pepper and the bay leaf. Bring the water to boiling point, lower the heat and simmer gently for a few minutes only, until the fish is cooked; do not over-cook, see page 48. Lift the fish from the liquid, drain carefully. Measure the liquid and add a little extra water if necessary to make 1 cup. Soften the gelatin in the sherry, stir into the hot fish liquid, stir until dissolved, then strain into a bowl. Chill until it begins to stiffen slightly, then fold in mayonnaise, flaked fish, and lightly whipped cream and chopped parsley. Taste and season with salt and pepper. Put into an oiled 1 quart bowl or mold and chill until set.

To serve:
To unmold, see Beef and Tomato Mold, page 113. Turn out on to a bed of mixed salad greens.
To freeze:
Do not freeze this dish, but frozen fish could be used.

Paella Salad

To make: 25 minutes   **To cook:** 20 minutes   **Serves 6–8**

1–2 cloves garlic
2 medium-sized onions
½ small chicken
3 tablespoons olive oil
1 cup long grain rice
2 cups chicken stock or water and 2
    chicken bouillon cubes
pinch saffron
¼–⅓ cup mayonnaise
½–1 tablespoon lemon juice
8–12 oz. cooked white fish (cod,
    flounder, haddock, halibut)
2 teaspoons chopped parsley
½–1 teaspoon chopped fennel
    (optional)
1 canned pimiento
1 cup cooked peas
1 cup cooked, shelled and deveined
    shrimp

Peel and chop the garlic and onions. Skin and bone the chicken. Cut the chicken into small pieces and sauté in the hot oil for a few minutes. Stir in garlic, onions and rice and sauté for 2–3 minutes. Mix the stock or water and bouillon cubes with the saffron, pour into the pan and stir well. Lower the heat, but do not cover the pan and simmer for about 15 minutes, until the rice is tender and has absorbed the liquid; stir once or twice during this period. Remove from the heat and add the mayonnaise and lemon juice while the mixture is hot. Cool, then fold in flaked fish, herbs, chopped pimiento, peas and shrimp. Chill.

To serve:
On a bed of salad greens.
To vary:
Paella: Proceed as the recipe above, but omit the mayonnaise and the lemon juice. Heat the fish, vegetables and herbs in the pan with the rice, and serve this as a hot dish. A greater selection of shellfish can be added, together with thinly sliced garlic sausage or pepperoni, and you can omit the white fish if desired. There are many recipes for this famous dish, varying with the region of Spain, but the rather unusual mixture of chicken, fish, etc. is a great success.
To freeze:
This is better served soon after cooking.
To economize:
This is a good way to use small quantities of chicken and fish to produce a satisfying dish.

Blue Cheese & Pear Salad

To make: 6–8 minutes   **No cooking**   **Serves 4**

8 oz. blue cheese
little mayonnaise (see method)
8 canned pear halves
1 head Boston lettuce
To garnish:
few grapes, seeded
Quick tip:
Use canned cherries in place of
grapes.

Crumble the cheese and blend with enough mayonnaise to make a creamy consistency. Arrange the pear halves rounded side up on a bed of lettuce leaves. Top with the cheese mixture and garnish with the grapes.
To serve:
As a light main dish.
To vary:
Add chopped nuts to the cheese mixture.
Use grated Cheddar cheese, mixed with seedless raisins, in place of blue cheese.
   Use halved fresh pears, sprinkled with lemon juice or French dressing, see page 110, to prevent their discoloring.
To freeze:
Do not freeze this dish.
To economize:
Use left-over grated cheese (see To vary).

Blue cheese and pear salad

Light Dishes

There are many occasions when a light quick dish is all that one requires for a meal. In the next pages you will find suggestions that are suitable for lunches, suppers or meals for the children. In most cases these are "one dish meals" which can be served with vegetables, but they can also be served simply accompanied by a salad, with toast or rolls and butter.

Economical light dishes: There are so many foods that can be served for a light luncheon or supper or a T.V. snack later at night, or for children's dishes.

Soups can form a complete meal if followed by cheese and fruit or some of the ideas given in the chapter on Appetizers, starting on page 12, are equally as good for a light complete meal as for an hors d'oeuvre. Some of the most economical foods upon which to base your light dishes are eggs and cheese. Both these foods are high in protein value. Remember it is important that light meals should be well balanced so check to see that the family is having essential vitamins in the form of fresh fruit and vegetables too. There are many economical ways in which you can add extra food value to the popular convenience foods, such as frozen fish sticks and hamburgers. Serve them with baked beans for extra protein and fresh tomatoes or salad for vitamins.

Serve a cheese sauce, as the recipe on page 54, with fish sticks; this adds protein and a lot more flavor too. A crisp green salad turns this into a complete light meal.

Top cooked hamburgers or other meat cakes with a slice of cheese, heat under the broiler or in the oven until the cheese bubbles and browns lightly. Serve with fresh or cooked tomatoes.

Toasted snacks: Poached or scrambled eggs, see page 122, Welsh rarebit, page 118, sautéed or broiled mushrooms, sardines, baked beans can be served on hot buttered toast. To make a complete meal serve raw or broiled tomatoes and green salad with the toasted dish or follow this with fresh fruit.

Most cheese and egg dishes are quick to prepare, easily made and satisfying and there are a number in this chapter, and throughout the book that would be a good choice for a light meal. Encourage children to enjoy cheese, as it contains calcium which is so important for the formation of strong teeth and bones.

Savory rice or pasta dishes are an ideal choice for a quick meal, there are a number in this book, see pages 81, 102, 114 and 128–131 in particular.

Duchesse potatoes: Blend a generous amount of butter or margarine with mashed potatoes, together with 1–2 egg yolks (use the whites in meringues). Spoon or pipe into fancy shapes on a flameproof dish; brown and heat under the broiler or in the oven when required. These freeze well, so are also ideal for special occasions.

Scalloped potatoes: Slice peeled potatoes thinly, put into a heatproof dish with seasoned milk to cover. Top with a little butter or margarine and bake in a very moderate oven, 325°F. rather like a milk pudding, for about 1¼–1½ hours. The creamy potato mixture blends with hot or cold dishes and the potatoes can be prepared earlier in the day.

French fried potatoes or potato chips — see index.

Cheese and tomato medley

Cheese & Tomato Medley

To make: 15 minutes　**To cook:** 20–25 minutes　**Serves 4–6**

2 onions
8 oz. bacon
4 oz. fresh mushrooms
4–6 large cooked potatoes
1 clove garlic
¼ cup butter
1 lb. tomatoes
6 tablespoons water
salt and pepper
1½ cups (6 oz.) grated Gouda or
　Edam cheese
Quick tip:
Use canned tomatoes, plus liquid
from the can; omit the water. You can
also use canned potatoes and
mushrooms.

Chop the peeled onions and bacon, slice the mushrooms and potatoes and crush the garlic. Sauté the onions and garlic in half the butter until quite soft (you will need a good-sized pan). Then add the remaining butter. Add the bacon and mushrooms and stir over the heat for 5–10 minutes. Stir in the halved or quartered tomatoes and water, then the potatoes and salt and pepper. Stir well and cook for a further 3 minutes. Mix in half of the grated cheese and as soon as it melts the medley is ready to serve.
To serve:
Sprinkle the rest of the cheese on top.
To vary:
Use other vegetables that are in season. This is an excellent dish to make in a fondue pan or table cooker.
To freeze:
This dish does not freeze, but it is a good way of making a quick meal from frozen vegetables.
To economize:
Use any left-over vegetables and left-over pieces of cheese.

Welsh Rarebit

To make: 10 minutes　**To cook:** 12 minutes　**Serves 4–8**

¼ cup butter or margarine
¼ cup flour
3 tablespoons milk
3–4 tablespoons beer or more milk
　(use the larger amount for a softer
　mixture)
½–1 teaspoon prepared mustard
salt and pepper
few drops Worcestershire sauce
2 cups (8 oz.) grated cheese (see
　opposite)
4 large slices toast

Heat half the butter or margarine in a saucepan, stir in the flour and cook for 2–3 minutes, stirring well. Gradually stir in the milk and beer, if using; as this is a very stiff mixture, keep the heat very low and stir until thick. Add the mustard, salt and pepper and Worcestershire sauce. Do not add the cheese over the heat, but remove from range and stir in the cheese. Good cooking cheeses are suggested opposite. Meanwhile toast the bread and spread with the remaining butter or margarine. Spread toast with Welsh rarebit mixture. Heat for 2–3 minutes under the broiler until golden.
To serve:
As a light lunch or supper dish with broiled tomatoes and/or salad or cut each slice in half and serve as a canapé or appetizer.

Cheese Pudding

To make: 10 minutes plus standing　**To bake:** 30–35 minutes　**Serves 4**

2 cups soft breadcrumbs
2 cups milk
2 tablespoons butter or margarine
2–3 eggs
2 cups (8 oz.) grated cheese, choose
　Cheddar, Gruyère or Emmenthal
salt and pepper
To garnish:
parsley
2 tomatoes

Put the breadcrumbs into a bowl. Heat milk with the butter or margarine until steaming. Pour milk over the crumbs and allow to stand for about 10 minutes; this is not essential but softens the breadcrumbs and produces a smoother mixture. Add beaten eggs, the third egg would give a lighter result, and grated cheese. Season with salt and pepper. Pour into a 1 quart shallow casserole or 9-inch pie plate and bake for 30–35 minutes in a moderately hot oven, 400°F.
To serve:
As soon as baked, topped with parsley and sliced tomato and with a green vegetable or salad.
To vary:
If baking in a rather deeper soufflé dish, use a slightly lower oven temperature and allow about 40 minutes cooking time. Add finely diced cooked ham or flaked fish to the mixture; do not add more than about ⅔ cup otherwise the pudding will not rise.
To freeze:
Do not freeze this dish, but it is a good idea to have a container of soft breadcrumbs in the freezer to use when required.
To economize:
This is a good way of using up left-over bread and rather dry cheese.

Cooking with Cheese

There are a great variety of cheeses on sale, but best to use for grating and cooking are Cheddar or Parmesan or the stronger Romano. Gruyère, Emmenthal, Dutch Gouda or Edam or processed cheeses are also excellent either chopped, grated or sliced.

Do not over-cook cheese, as this makes it tough and rather stringy. When making a cheese sauce, cook the white sauce, see page 54, add the cheese, remove from heat and stir until the cheese has melted or reheat for a very short time only.

Cheese Dreams

To make: 5 minutes   **To cook:** 5 minutes   **Serves 2**

4–6 large slices bread
little butter
2–3 slices processed or Cheddar cheese
1 egg
3 tablespoons milk
salt and pepper
To fry:
¼ cup fat, butter or margarine
To garnish:
tomatoes (see method)

Make sandwiches with the bread, butter and cheese. Cut into fingers. Beat the egg with milk and salt and pepper. Pour into a pie plate. Heat the fat, butter or margarine in a frying pan; make sure it is not too hot. Dip each sandwich into the egg and milk for a few seconds only, if left too long they will become soft and break. Fry for 1–2 minutes on either side until crisp and brown.
To serve:
As soon as cooked with raw or fried halved tomatoes.
To vary:
Spread the bread and butter with mustard, ketchup or pickle relish. Put slices of ham as well as cheese into the sandwiches.
To freeze:
The cooked dish cannot be frozen, but frozen sandwiches could be coated like this then fried. If you are planning a picnic or other occasion where you need to prepare a lot of sandwiches, make these, then wrap and freeze. Use within 1 month; do not use hard-cooked egg or crisp salad ingredients in the filling.
To economize:
Even very stale bread and dry cheese becomes appetizing when cooked like this.

Cheese & Bacon

To make: 5 minutes   **To cook:** 8–10 minutes   **Serves 4**

4 slices bread
a little butter
8 slices bacon
8 slices Cheddar or Samsoe cheese
To garnish:
8 tomatoes
salt and pepper
few gherkins (optional)
Quick tip:
Cover broiler pan with foil to ease washing-up.

Toast the bread and spread with butter. Broil bacon until crisp. Cover the toast with the cheese and broil until it bubbles. Broil the halved tomatoes, sprinkled with salt and pepper. Top the toast with the bacon and garnish with the tomatoes and gherkins, if desired.
To serve:
As a light main dish; also good for breakfast.
To vary:
Top with a poached egg instead of bacon.
To freeze:
Do not freeze this dish, but sliced bread may be toasted right from the freezer.
To economize:
Use left-over grated cheese instead of sliced cheese.

Cheese and bacon

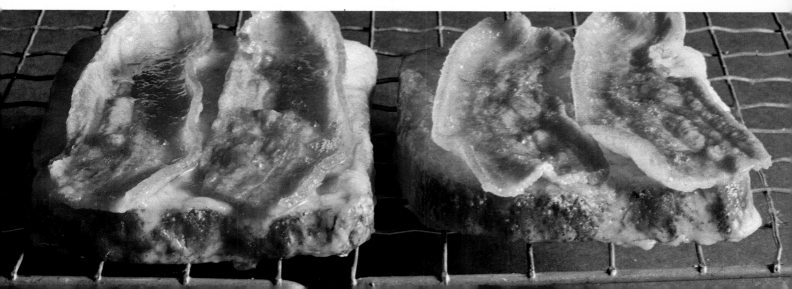

Cauliflower basket

Cauliflower Basket

To make: 20 minutes   **To cook:** 20–25 minutes   **Serves 4–6**

1 medium-sized cauliflower
salt
For the cheese sauce:
2 tablespoons butter or margarine
¼ cup flour
⅔ cup milk
⅔ cup liquid from cooking the
    cauliflower (see method)
salt and pepper
1 cup (4 oz.) grated Cheddar cheese
2 eggs
1 tablespoon chopped gherkins
1 teaspoon capers
1 tablespoon chopped parsley
1 tablespoon chopped chives
Quick tip:
Break cauliflower into flowerets and
cook for 7–8 minutes only. Put into a
heated serving dish, top with sauce
mixture and brown under the broiler.

Trim the cauliflower, keeping it whole. Cook in boiling salted water to
cover until just tender, drain, reserving ⅔ cup of the cooking liquid. While
the cauliflower is cooking, prepare the sauce. Heat the butter or margarine
in a saucepan, stir in the flour and cook over low heat for 2–3 minutes,
stirring well. Gradually stir in the milk, bring to a boil, then stir in the
reserved cauliflower liquid and stir as the sauce thickens over medium
heat. Remove from the heat and add salt and pepper and nearly all the
cheese. Hard-cook the eggs, shell and chop. Stir eggs into hot cheese
sauce, along with the gherkins, capers and herbs. Scoop out the center part
of the cauliflower. Place cauliflower removed on a plate, chop coarsely and
add to the sauce. Stand the hollowed cauliflower in a heated serving dish.
Spoon the cheese sauce mixture into the center. Top with the remaining
cheese and brown for 1–2 minutes under a broiler.
To serve:
Hot as a light main course with tomato salad or with meat, fish or poultry.
To vary:
Omit the eggs and use cooked shelled and deveined shrimp or diced
cooked ham instead.
   This dish can be adapted as a cold salad dish.
   Cook the cauliflower as described in the method above, but be extra
careful when cooking the vegetable that it does not become too soft, for it
should have a firm texture when cold. Stir grated cheese into mayonnaise
instead of a white sauce, add the chopped hard-cooked eggs, gherkins,
capers and herbs. Spoon over the hot cauliflower, then allow to cool.
To freeze:
Do not freeze this dish if possible, although frozen cauliflower flowerets
could be used.
To economize:
Use left-over cheese for the sauce. Dry cheese grates well and is quite
suitable for cooking, providing it is the type that does melt easily.

Creamed Fish with Anchovies

To make: 15 minutes   **To cook:** 15–20 minutes   **Serves 4**

1½ lbs. haddock or cod fillets
salt and pepper
6 tablespoons butter or margarine
6 canned flat anchovy fillets
2–3 small onions
3 tomatoes
1½ tablespoons chopped parsley
⅔ cup heavy or light cream or
    evaporated milk

Quick tip:
Use well drained canned tomatoes
and instant minced onion.

Cut the fish into pieces, season with salt and pepper. Melt ¼ cup of the butter or margarine in a saucepan, add the chopped anchovies and cook gently for 2 minutes. Add the coarsely chopped onions and quartered tomatoes and cook gently for a further 5 minutes. Stir in the parsley and spoon the hot mixture into a flameproof dish. Place the fish pieces on top, dot with the remaining butter or margarine and broil until brown, about 7–10 minutes. Turn the fish and broil another 8 minutes. Spoon the cream over the fish and broil another 5 minutes.

To serve:
With cooked rice, pasta or Duchesse potatoes above; this is particularly good with the Crispy Fried Noodles on page 131.

To freeze:
While you can freeze the cooked dish, it is better to serve it when freshly cooked. Frozen fish can be used.

To economize:
Light cream can be used in the recipe above or rich milk.

Cheese Soufflé

To make: 15 minutes   **To bake:** 30–35 minutes   **Serves 4**

1 cup (4 oz.) Cheddar, Gruyère,
    Parmesan or Gouda cheese*
2 tablespoons butter or margarine
¼ cup flour
⅔ cup milk
salt and pepper
4 eggs or 3 egg yolks and 4 egg whites
*Do not exceed this amount.

Quick tip:
Make up nearly 1¼ cups instant mashed potatoes, add the cheese then the eggs as the recipe.

To vary:
Chicken soufflés: Use ground chicken and chicken stock instead of cheese and milk.

Fish soufflés: Use finely chopped or flaked cooked or canned fish (white fish, shellfish or oily fish such as salmon) instead of cheese.

Meat soufflés: Use finely chopped or ground cooked ham, cooked liver or cooked tongue and stock or stock mixed with milk instead of cheese and milk.

Vegetable soufflés: Use vegetable puree, tomato or spinach are particularly good, instead of milk. A little cheese can be added to the mixture.

To economize:
This is a fairly inexpensive, but a very nutritious and satisfying dish.

Grate the cheese finely. Heat the butter or margarine in a large saucepan, stir in the flour and cook over low heat for several minutes. Gradually stir in the milk over medium heat until sauce becomes really thick. Remove from heat, add salt and pepper and cheese. Separate the eggs and beat the yolks into the cheese mixture. Cool. Beat the whites until they are almost as stiff as a meringue; if they are beaten too much until they are very stiff the soufflé rises dramatically, but may be a little dry. Pour into a buttered 1 quart soufflé dish. Bake in a moderate to moderately hot oven, 375–400°F. for 30–35 minutes. Serve at once.

Cheese soufflé

Cooking with Eggs

Eggs are an essential ingredient in many recipes, but they also form the basis for many quick and easy dishes on their own.

Remember practically all hot egg dishes should be served as soon as they are cooked, waiting will spoil them. The basic ways of cooking eggs are given below, for many seemingly elaborate dishes are based upon these methods.

To freeze:
Many dishes containing eggs freeze well, but cooked whole eggs cannot be frozen as they become tough.

Basic Ways to Cook Eggs

Baked eggs:
Butter individual ovenproof dishes, break eggs into these and top with a little milk or light or heavy cream and salt and pepper. Bake for about 10 minutes in a moderately hot oven, 375–400°F. until eggs are set. This is only the beginning of an interesting dish, you can add grated cheese, chopped ham, asparagus tips, shrimp, etc.

Boiled eggs:
Lower the eggs into boiling water, allow 3½–4 minutes for soft-cooked eggs or up to 10 minutes for hard-cooked eggs.

Fried eggs:
Make sure the butter or margarine is hot before adding the eggs to the frying pan. Break the egg on a saucer (then slide into the fat), or break eggs one at a time right into the hot butter. Lower the heat slightly and fry until set for sunnyside-up eggs. For eggs over-easy, turn eggs with a pancake turner and fry for another 1–2 minutes.

Poached eggs:
Either heat small pieces of butter or margarine in metal egg poacher cups, then add the eggs and poach for about 3 minutes over boiling water or heat salted water in a pan; add a few drops of vinegar to keep the eggs a good shape (this is not essential). One at a time, break the eggs into a cup (then slide into the water), or break right into the water and simmer for 2–3 minutes. A slotted spoon is ideal to slide under the egg and lift it out of the liquid.

Scrambled eggs:
Beat the eggs very lightly with salt and pepper and add 1 teaspoon milk or light cream for each egg. Heat a piece of butter or margarine in a pan, add the eggs and stir gently over low heat until just set. Do not over-cook, as the eggs continue to set in the heat of the pan.

Quiche Lorraine

To make: 25 minutes **To bake:** 1 hour 20 minutes **Serves 4–6**

For the pie crust:
1½ cups all-purpose flour
pinch salt
6 tablespoons vegetable shortening
water to mix
For the filling:
8 slices bacon
1½ cups (6 oz.) grated Cheddar or
   Gruyère cheese
3 eggs
1¼ cups milk
6 tablespoons light cream or half and
   half
salt and pepper
To garnish:
lettuce
tomato

Sift the flour and salt, cut in the shortening until the mixture resembles fine breadcrumbs. Add enough water to make a firm dough. Roll out and line an 8-inch pie or flan pan (at least 1½ inches in depth). Line pan with waxed paper and fill with beans or rice and bake for about 18–20 minutes in a hot oven, 400–425°F. until golden colored and set; do not overcook. The paper and beans or rice should be removed after 15 minutes. Save the rice or beans in a canister for the next pie baking.

To prepare the filling, fry or broil the bacon lightly, do not overcook. Chop finely. Put at the bottom of the flan shell. Grate the cheese and sprinkle over bacon. Beat the eggs with milk, cream and salt and pepper. Pour egg mixture over the bacon. Bake for about 50 minutes — 1 hour in a slow oven, 325°F. until firm to the touch.

To serve:
Hot or cold, garnished with lettuce and tomato slices.

To freeze:
This freezes well for some weeks, but you must use nearly all light cream instead of milk and cream. Freeze pie before baking and bake from frozen state.

Oeufs florentine

Oeufs Florentine

To make: 30 minutes   **To bake:** 10–15 minutes   **Serves 4**

1 lb. fresh spinach
salt and pepper
3 tablespoons butter
¼ cup flour
1¼ cups milk
⅔ cup grated Parmesan or Cheddar
  cheese
4 eggs
3–4 tablespoons light cream
To garnish:
tomato slices
Quick tip:
Use frozen chopped spinach, thawed
and squeezed dry.

Wash the spinach well, put it into a pan with a little salt and just the water that clings to the leaves. Cover and cook for 10–15 minutes, until tender, then drain well. Chop roughly and mix with 1 tablespoon of the butter and salt and pepper. Put into a shallow baking dish. Meanwhile make a cheese sauce, melt the remaining butter in a pan, stir in the flour and cook over low heat for 1 minute. Gradually stir in milk and stir until thickened. Cook for 2 minutes. Stir in ½ cup of the cheese; do not cook again. Poach the eggs lightly, see opposite, and place side by side on the spinach. Stir cream into the cheese sauce and pour over the spinach and eggs, sprinkle with the remaining cheese. Put the dish in a moderate oven, 375°F. and bake for 10–15 minutes until golden. Alternatively, brown in broiler. Garnish with tomato slices.

To serve:
As a light main dish.
To vary:
Cook the eggs in the shell instead of poaching them. You can have soft or hard-cooked according to personal taste.
To freeze:
Do not freeze this dish, but you can use frozen spinach.
To economize:
If spinach is expensive, use kale or other cheaper green vegetable such as mustard or collard greens.

123

Egg & Tomato Pie

To make: 20 minutes   **To bake:** 45 minutes   **Serves 4**

2 large onions
¼ cup butter
1 lb. tomatoes
2 cups soft breadcrumbs
salt and pepper
4 eggs
To garnish:
parsley

Peel the onions then slice them and fry lightly in 3 tablespoons of the butter. Skin and slice the tomatoes. Butter a shallow baking dish and fill it with alternate layers of the fried onions and tomatoes, sprinkling each layer with a few of the breadcrumbs and salt and pepper. Finish with a thick layer of the crumbs, dot with pieces of the remaining butter and bake in a moderate oven, 350–375°F. for 45 minutes. Poach the eggs just before the pie is baked.

To serve:
Top with the eggs and garnish with parsley.

To freeze:
The vegetable mixture can be frozen, but not the poached eggs. Use within 3 months.

French Omelet

To make: few minutes   **To cook:** 4–5 minutes   **Serves 2**

4 eggs
salt and pepper
1 tablespoon water
3 tablespoons butter

Beat the eggs with salt and pepper and the water very lightly; there is no need to do more than blend the yolks and whites. Heat the butter in an 8-inch skillet or omelet pan (do not use a larger pan otherwise the mixture will be too thinly spread over the bottom). Pour in the eggs and leave for about ½–1 minute, until set at the bottom, then loosen the eggs with a spatula away from the side of the pan, tilting pan at the same time to allow uncooked egg to run underneath. Continue lifting edge of omelet until just set, or even a little liquid in the center. Fold omelet away from the handle with a spatula. Slide on to a hot plate and serve at once.

To vary:
Fry diced bread or cooked potatoes in the butter, add the eggs and continue as above. The omelet will then serve 3–4 people. Fill with grated cheese, cooked fish, sautéed chicken livers, chopped chicken see page 81, before folding.

Flavor the eggs with chopped herbs, sliced sautéed mushrooms, or finely chopped ham before cooking.

Kidney omelet

Soufflé Omelet

This type of omelet is made differently from the French or plain omelet opposite. Separate the egg yolks from the whites and put the yolks into a bowl. Although soufflé omelets are often served as a dessert, you can also use this lighter type of mixture with a savory filling. Add salt and pepper or 1 tablespoon sugar to each 3–4 egg yolks plus 1 tablespoon milk or cream (heavy or light). Beat together. Beat the egg whites until they stand up in peaks then fold into the yolks. Heat 3 tablespoons butter in an 8-inch omelet pan. Pour in the egg mixture and cook over low to moderate heat until just set at the bottom. Meanwhile heat the broiler. Place the omelet pan under the broiler 6–8 inches away from source of heat. When the omelet is just set, mark across the center with a knife (this makes the omelet easier to fold). Spread with the filling, fold and place on a hot dish. The picture shows a sweet omelet filled and topped with halved strawberries and hot strawberry jam, or you could use redcurrant jelly.

Soufflé omelet

Oven Baked Omelet

To make: 10 minutes   **To bake:** 15–20 minutes   **Serves 3–4**

½ cup cooked vegetables
⅓ cup grated cheese, or chopped cooked ham or chicken
¼ cup butter
4–6 eggs
salt and pepper
Quick tip:
Use left-over vegetables and meat, or open a small can deviled ham, chicken, roast beef or liver spread.

In a bowl, mix the diced vegetables with the grated cheese, diced ham or chicken. Put the butter into an 8-inch round shallow baking dish and heat this for 2–3 minutes in the oven until melted. Stir in vegetable mixture. Stir in well beaten eggs and salt and pepper. Bake in a moderate to moderately hot oven, 375–400°F. for a little over 15 minutes until just set.
To serve:
As soon as it is cooked.
To vary:
Any fillings used for omelets can be adapted for this type of cooking. If you prefer a soufflé type omelet prepare as the recipe above, warm the filling in the dish, pour the egg mixture over the filling and bake as above. Do not over-cook, as this would spoil the texture of the eggs.

125

Spanish omelet

Spanish Omelet

To make: 15 minutes   **To cook:** 10 minutes   **Serves 2**

1 small onion
3 small cooked potatoes
1 canned pimiento
1 large tomato
1 clove garlic
3 tablespoons oil
3–4 tablespoons cooked peas
3 eggs
½ teaspoon Tabasco
salt and pepper
pinch fines herbes
Quick tip:
Prepare all the vegetables earlier,
keep in a covered container until
ready to cook the omelet.

Chop the peeled onion finely, dice the potatoes, pepper and skinned
tomato (discard seeds if possible). Crush the garlic. Heat 1 tablespoon of
the oil in the pan and sauté the onion and garlic until soft. Add the
remaining oil, heat, then stir in remaining vegetables and heat thoroughly.
Meanwhile, beat the eggs lightly, add Tabasco and salt and pepper and
pour into the pan over the vegetables. Stir lightly, then cook until the eggs
are just set. Do not turn omelet. Sprinkle with herbs just before serving.
To serve:
Immediately after cooking. Do not fold like most omelets. This makes an
excellent main dish with salad or green vegetables.
To vary:
Add small pieces of left-over ham, fish, poultry or other meat, etc.
To freeze:
One cannot freeze an omelet, but I find it useful to freeze small containers
of mixed cooked vegetables.
To economize:
Use up any left-over vegetables or meat in this dish.

Savory Egg Custard

To make: 10 minutes   **To bake:** 1 hour   **Serves 3–4**

3–4 eggs
salt and pepper
2½ cups milk or half milk and half
   stock
1½ cups (6 oz.) grated cheese or
   cooked ham or skinned raw fish

Beat the eggs with salt and pepper. Stir in milk or milk and stock, then stir
in the grated cheese, diced ham or fish. Spoon into a shallow baking dish
and stand in cold water as described on page 145. Bake for 1 hour or until
set in a slow oven, 275–300°F. If more convenient, steam for the same
length of time.
To serve:
Hot or cold with thin bread and butter; this is an easily digested dish.

Eggs Pipérade

To make: 10 minutes   **To cook:** 10–15 minutes   **Serves 2–4**

1–2 onions
1–2 cloves garlic (optional)
2–3 tomatoes
1 green pepper
¼ cup butter or 2 tablespoons butter
    and 1 tablespoon oil
4–6 eggs
salt and pepper
To garnish:
toast

Peel and chop the onions, chop or crush the garlic, if using, skin and chop the tomatoes and chop the green pepper (discard seeds). Heat the butter or butter and oil in a pan, add the vegetables and sauté until tender. Beat the eggs with salt and pepper. Pour over vegetables, lower the heat and stir gently until just set, see page 122 for comments about scrambling eggs.
To serve:
Although this can be served cold as an hors d'oeuvre or main dish, I think it is better hot; serve immediately it is cooked, garnished with toast.
To freeze:
Although scrambled eggs cannot be frozen, it is a good idea to freeze small packages of cooked vegetables, reheat, then continue as above.

Egg & Cheese Pie

To make: 15 minutes   **To bake:** 20–25 minutes   **Serves 4–6**

6–8 eggs
salt and pepper
1¼ cups cheese sauce (see page 54)
1 lb. seasoned mashed potatoes
½ cup (2 oz.) grated cheese

Hard-cook then halve the eggs lengthwise, put them into a shallow baking dish, cover with the well seasoned cheese sauce and pipe a border of mashed potato around the dish. Top with grated cheese and bake in a moderately hot oven 375–400°F. for about 20–25 minutes.
To serve:
With green salad, cooked cauliflower or mixed vegetables.
To vary:
Mix diced cooked vegetables or crumbled crisp bacon slices with the cheese sauce.
To freeze:
This dish cannot be frozen.

Surprise Scotch Eggs

To make: 20 minutes   **To cook:** 20–25 minutes   **Serves 4**

4 eggs
2 tablespoons butter
½ cup (2 oz.) grated Parmesan cheese
½–1 teaspoon prepared mustard
salt and pepper
1–2 tablespoons flour
12 oz. bulk sausage
1 egg
⅔ cup dry breadcrumbs
To fry:
deep fat or oil

Hard-cook the eggs for just 10 minutes, crack the shells and plunge into cold water; this prevents a dark line forming around the yolks. Remove the shells, halve the eggs lengthwise and remove the yolks. Reserve egg whites. Mash yolks with the butter, then add the cheese, mustard and salt and pepper. Spoon back into the egg whites. Press the two halves together again and coat with flour mixed with salt and pepper. Divide the sausage into 4 pieces, press out each piece on a floured board and wrap around the eggs, molding this carefully into a smooth coating. Coat in flour mixed with salt and pepper, then in beaten egg and crumbs. Fry slowly for 10–12 minutes in the hot fat or oil, see page 44 for details of testing the fat or oil. Drain on absorbent paper.
To serve:
Hot or cold with salads or vegetables.
To vary:
Scotch eggs: Do not flavor the eggs, simply hard-cook and coat as above, then fry.
To freeze:
Never try to freeze this dish, the eggs will be tough.
To economize:
Use well seasoned thick mashed potato instead of bulk sausage.

Stuffed Tomatoes

To make: 10 minutes   **To bake:** 10–15 minutes   **Serves 4**

4 large or 8 medium-sized tomatoes
2 eggs
½ cup (2 oz.) grated cheese
salt and pepper
2 teaspoons chopped gherkins
2 tablespoons butter
To garnish:
French or Belgian endive or
    watercress

Cut a thin slice off bottom of each tomato to allow tomatoes to stand straight. Core tomatoes. Slice off top of tomato. Scoop out the center pulp leaving a shell about ½-inch thick. Chop pulp removed and stir in beaten eggs, cheese, salt and pepper and gherkins. Spoon this mixture into the tomato cases, replace the "lids" and put into a shallow buttered baking dish, top each tomato with a little butter. Bake for 10–15 minutes in a moderate oven 375°F.
To serve:
As soon as cooked garnished with French or Belgian endive or watercress.

Pasta

Pasta, i.e., spaghetti, macaroni, noodles, etc. have become very popular today. They are inexpensive and easy to store and can be combined with many different foods.

Secrets of cooking pasta:
There are two golden rules, the first is never to over-cook the pasta, particularly if it is being reheated with other ingredients, as the macaroni cheese on page 130 or the fried noodles on page 131.

The second point to remember is to use plenty of water to cook the pasta for if you use too little it becomes sticky. Allow 5 cups water to each 4 oz. pasta; make sure the water is boiling BEFORE the pasta is added, and keep the water boiling constantly throughout the cooking period. With long pasta, such as spaghetti, it is advisable to keep it moving in the boiling water, by lifting it with two spoons to prevent it from sticking. Test the pasta by pressing gently, but firmly, against the side of a pan; the pasta is cooked when it breaks with light pressure. The Italians call it "al dente" which means it is just firm to bite, but not over-soft. Drain the pasta, you may like to rinse it in boiling water to get rid of any starchy coating, but this is not essential if you have cooked it correctly.

Cooked pasta can just be tossed in melted butter and chopped parsley or grated cheese and melted butter and served instead of potatoes with main dishes.

To freeze:
While you can cook a large amount of pasta, use what you want and freeze the rest, this does seem pointless as it is so quick and easy to prepare. It is however, worth preparing and freezing dishes such as Spaghetti Bolognese and Spaghetti alla Napolitaine below.

Some interesting pasta shapes:
In addition to the more familiar macaroni and spaghetti look for cannelloni (like giant macaroni) or giant shells. Cook, fill with a meat mixture, such as the filling for Beef Stuffed Crêpes, page 78. Top with white or cheese sauce, page 55 and heat.

Buy bow-ties, ziti, elbows or rotelli, cook, then toss in butter and parsley, and serve instead of potatoes, or mix with mayonnaise and diced cheese for a salad. Fine noodles make an excellent accompaniment to dishes, especially when fried, see page 131.

Spaghetti alla Napolitaine

To make: 15 minutes   **To cook:** 15 minutes   **Serves 4–5**

8 oz. spaghetti
salt and pepper
little grated Parmesan cheese (see method)
little butter (see method)
1 can (14 oz.) tomatoes (preferably plum type)
1 tablespoon tomato paste
4 oz. chopped cooked ham
little chopped parsley
Quick tip:
Use prepared marinara sauce with ham added.

Cook the spaghetti in boiling salted water (allow at least 7½ cups water to the smaller quantity of pasta) until tender. Drain then toss with the Parmesan cheese and butter. Meanwhile heat the canned tomatoes with the tomato paste, stir in diced ham, parsley and salt and pepper. Spoon the spaghetti on a hot dish and top with the tomato sauce.
To serve:
Hot with plenty of grated cheese or a green salad. This also makes a good hors d'oeuvre.
To vary:
Spaghetti à la Reine: Cook the spaghetti as above, drain, return to pan, add a little butter, diced cooked chicken, enough beef stock to moisten and grated cheese. Heat for a few minutes then serve with more grated cheese.
To freeze:
Pasta tends to lose some of its texture when frozen, so use within 4–6 weeks. Cook, drain, then rinse in cold water; mix with the cheese and butter, pack and freeze. Freeze the tomato mixture separately.
To economize:
Use small pieces of left-over cooked meat, chicken or fish instead of ham.

Spaghetti alla napolitaine

Macaroni Cheese

To make: 15–20 minutes   **To bake:** 25 minutes   **Serves 4**

3 oz. elbow macaroni
salt
1¼ cups cheese sauce (see page 54)
½ cup (2 oz.) grated cheese
1 tablespoon dry breadcrumbs
2 tablespoons margarine or butter
To garnish:
tomato

Put the macaroni into about 3¾ cups boiling water, with a teaspoon salt. Cook until the macaroni is just tender. Do not over-cook; quick-cooking elbow macaroni takes only 7 minutes. Drain well, mix with the sauce. Pour mixture into a shallow baking dish. Sprinkle the cheese and breadcrumbs on top and dot with the margarine or butter. Either bake for about 25 minutes in a moderately hot oven, 400°F. until crisp and brown, or put under a hot broiler. Garnish with tomato slices.

To vary:
If the dish is to stand or if you prefer a more moist mixture, use sauce made with 2 cups milk, etc.

To economize:
Use half milk and half chicken broth.

Spaghetti with Anchovies

To make: 20 minutes   **To cook:** 20 minutes   **Serves 4**

4 oz. spaghetti
salt
¼ cup olive oil
8 oz. fresh mushrooms
2 onions
2 cloves garlic
5 anchovy fillets
3 slices lean bacon
6 black olives
little roughly chopped parsley
3–4 tablespoons grated Parmesan
    cheese

Cook the spaghetti in boiling salted water (allow 4 cups water) until tender; drain. Meanwhile, heat the oil in a heavy skillet. Add the sliced mushrooms and onions, crushed garlic, chopped anchovy fillets and bacon, olives and parsley, and cook gently for about 15 minutes.

To serve:
Top the spaghetti with the anchovy mixture and grated Parmesan cheese.

To vary:
Spaghetti maré: Omit the bacon and add flaked tuna fish and cooked, shelled shrimp.

To freeze:
This dish is better eaten when freshly made.

Spaghetti with anchovies

Fried Crispy Noodles

To make: 5–6 minutes   **To cook:** 10 minutes   **Serves 4**

4 oz. fine noodles
salt
To fry:
deep fat or oil heated to 380°F.
To economize:
Cook and fry a good quantity of noodles for these are an inexpensive and interesting food. Freeze excess.

Cook the noodles in boiling salted water (allow 7½ cups) for 5 minutes only. Drain, rinse with cold water and drain again until really dry on paper towels. Place in a heated frying basket in hot fat or oil, see page 44 for the way to test the temperature of oil. Fry for 5 minutes or until crisp and golden brown. Drain well on absorbent paper and keep hot until required.
To serve:
With most main dishes instead of potatoes.
To vary:
Fried rice: Choose long grain rice, boil until nearly soft, see page 66, then rinse as above. Fry in a little oil or butter and oil in a frying pan until golden.
To freeze:
Spread out on a flat tray in a single layer and freeze until hard. This prevents the fried noodles sticking to the wrapping. Pack when frozen. Use within 2 months. To reheat spread out on a cookie sheet, do not cover, and warm through in a hot oven 400°F. for a few minutes only. Drain on absorbent paper.

Spaghetti with Ham & Mushrooms

To make: 15 minutes   **To cook:** 15–20 minutes   **Serves 4**

6 oz. spaghetti
salt and pepper
8 oz. fresh mushrooms
¼ cup butter
4 oz. chopped cooked ham or tongue
1 small onion
To garnish:
olives

Cook the spaghetti in boiling salted water (allow 6 cups) until tender, drain. Meanwhile sauté the sliced mushrooms in the hot butter until tender, add the diced ham or tongue and the finely chopped or grated onion and continue to cook until slightly brown. Mix with the spaghetti and add salt and pepper to taste.
To serve:
On a hot dish, garnished with olives.
To freeze:
This dish is better eaten when freshly made.

Spaghetti Bolognese

To make: 25 minutes   **To cook:** 1 hour   **Serves 4–6**

Ingredients as the filling for the Beef Stuffed Crêpes (see page 78)

1–2 cloves garlic
2–3 large tomatoes
1 onion
10 oz. spaghetti
salt
grated Parmesan cheese (see method)

Prepare the meat mixture as the filling for the crêpes on page 78, but sauté the finely chopped garlic and skinned, chopped tomatoes with the chopped onion. Simmer sauce until the meat is tender, about 40–45 minutes. About 15–20 minutes before the end of the cooking time put the spaghetti into boiling salted water (allow 8–10 cups water) and cook until tender, drain.
To serve:
Top the spaghetti with the meat sauce and serve with the cheese.
To freeze:
See the comments under Spaghetti alla Napolitaine, page 128.

Tagliatelle with Tomato Sauce

To make: 20 minutes   **To cook:** 25 minutes   **Serves 4–5**

For the tomato sauce:
1 lb. tomatoes
2 onions
1 clove garlic
¼ cup butter or margarine
1¼ cups water
3 tablespoons tomato paste
salt and pepper

8 oz. tagliatelle

Skin and chop the tomatoes, peel and chop the onions and garlic. Sauté the vegetables in the hot butter or margarine. Add the water, cover the pan and simmer for 15 minutes. Sieve or whirl in the blender, then return to the saucepan with the purée and salt and pepper. Meanwhile cook the tagliatelle (ribbon type noodles) in boiling salted water (allow 8 cups water) until tender, drain.
To serve:
Top pasta with tomato sauce and serve with grated cheese or main dishes.
To vary:
Use fettucini or medium width noodles.
To freeze:
See comments under Spaghetti alla Napolitaine, page 128. Use tomato sauce within 6 months.

Desserts

The selection of foods served as a dessert has become much more versatile during the last years, as we enjoy more cakes as a change from the heavy puddings. You will find most kinds of recipes covered in this section, together with advice on freezing that particular type of dish. The rather more special occasion desserts are at the beginning of this chapter, commencing with an early American syllabub.

Economical Puddings: One of the best ways to make economical puddings is to utilize fresh fruit when in season. I like to fill crêpes with a hot fruit purée or make a delicious Danish fruit pudding. Make about 3 cups coarse breadcrumbs. Fry crumbs until crisp in ¼ cup butter. Cool, then mix with 6 tablespoons sugar. Spoon crumbs on top of a thick fruit purée in a shallow bowl, press neatly until flat on top. Chill and serve with cream. If preferred, put half the crumbs into the serving dish, top with the fruit purée, then the rest of the crumbs. Use apple sauce, cooked dried fruits, crushed pineapple for the fruit purée.

To freeze: The method of freezing desserts will vary with the particular dish and you will find information given under the various recipes in this section.

It is helpful to have a selection of desserts in your freezer, and often it is so easy to make double, triple or even larger quantities of a pudding, pie or ice cream, enjoy some when freshly cooked and freeze the rest.

Freeze raw and cooked fruit to use throughout the year. Purées of fruit are particularly useful, for they can be used for sauces over ice cream, as well as the basis for other hot or cold puddings.

I like a selection of fruit pies in the freezer. The pastry may be pre-cooked or just made then baked when desired.

Steamed sponge puddings freeze very well indeed. If you cook the puddings, freeze, then turn out of the pans and wrap firmly. Put back into the pans when you want to serve these, allow to thaw out to room temperature then heat thoroughly. The pudding is just as light as when freshly cooked. If more convenient you can mix the pudding, put into the pan, freeze and store. Thaw out thoroughly and steam in the usual way.

Crêpes are a wonderful "stand-by" in the freezer for they can be used as the basis for both main dish and sweet dishes. Separate each crêpe with foil or waxed paper, then the crêpes can be separated easily. Wrap in heavy duty foil and freeze. Just take the number of crêpes desired, heat then fill.

Decorated cakes are a most popular form of dessert. These take a considerable time to prepare and yet they freeze wonderfully. Always freeze the cake before covering, then wrap carefully, but thoroughly. Unwrap while still frozen, put on the serving dish and allow to thaw out for several hours at room temperature. In this way you do not spoil the appearance.

One would expect ice cream to freeze well and home-made ice cream is both a nutritious and delicious dessert. The recipe on page 136 is a good basic one and easily adaptable.

Berry pudding

Berry Pudding

To make: 30 minutes plus chilling   **To cook:** 15 minutes   **Serves 4–6**

1 pint strawberries, hulled
8 oz. dark sweet cherries, pitted
1 cooking apple, peeled, cored and
   sliced
½ cup sugar
sliced white or raisin bread (see
   method)
To decorate:
extra fruit (optional)
Quick tip:
Use ready sliced bread or cut unsliced
loaf lengthwise.

Put the fruit in a pan. Cover and heat gently until the juice leaves the fruit, stirring constantly to prevent the fruit from sticking. Crush the fruit slightly with a wooden spoon. Stir in sugar to taste. Butter the inside of a 1 quart heatproof bowl and line with thin slices of crustless bread or raisin bread. Fill with layers of warm fruit and bread ending with bread level with the top of the bowl. Butter the bottom of a small plate or saucer that will fit into the top of the bowl. Place it on top of the pudding and put a weight on top of this. Chill overnight.

To serve:
Unmold and garnish with additional fruit. If desired, thicken fruit juice with cornstarch to make a sauce. Serve with cream.

To vary:
Try rhubarb or other fruit. This makes a more attractive dessert if some red or dark fruit is used. If the fruit is very firm add a little water when cooking.

To freeze:
This freezes well. Chill before freezing. Use within 6 months.

To economize:
Use the most inexpensive fruit available.

Cherry Compote

To make: 10 minutes   **To cook:** 15 minutes   **Serves 6–8**

1½ lbs. bing cherries
⅔ cup red wine or dry sherry
¼ cup redcurrant or apple jelly
1 tablespoon sugar
grated rind and juice of 1 orange
pinch ground cinnamon
1 tablespoon arrowroot or cornstarch
3 tablespoons cold water
Quick tip:
Use canned fruit and add a little wine,
jelly and orange rind and juice.

Pit the cherries with the point of a vegetable peeler. Place the red wine or sherry, jelly, sugar, orange rind, juice and cinnamon into a pan. Cover and heat gently until the jelly is melted. Add the cherries, cover and simmer for 5 minutes. Mix arrowroot or cornstarch to a smooth paste with cold water. Stir into the cherries and bring to a boil, stirring continuously. Cool and serve at room temperature.

To vary:
Use apricots, pears, plums or peaches instead of cherries, but simmer for 15 minutes instead of 5 minutes.

To freeze:
Although this dish can be frozen, the flavor of the wine tends to be "lost" so freeze cherries in a plain syrup then add the wine etc. when serving.

To economize:
Mix apple slices or diced rhubarb with the cherries.

Crêpes aux Pommes

To make: 15 minutes   **To cook:** 20 minutes   **Serves 4–6**

1¼ cups water
¼ cup sugar
3 medium-sized cooking apples
batter made with 1 cup all-purpose
   flour, pinch salt, 2 eggs, 1¼ cups
   milk, 1 tablespoon oil or melted
   butter (see page 137)
For the sauce:
¼ cup butter
juice of 1 orange
¼ cup sugar
¼ cup Cointreau or brandy
To decorate:
grated orange rind
Quick tip:
Use canned apple pie filling.

Heat the water and sugar in a large pan. Peel, core and slice the apples and cook in the sugar syrup until tender. Make the crêpes as page 137 and fold each around several drained apple slices. Use any leftover syrup in a sauce, drink or fruit salad dressing. Melt the butter in a chafing dish or skillet, add the orange juice and sugar and simmer for 4–5 minutes. Add filled crêpes, pour the liqueur over and heat through. Sprinkle with orange rind and serve at once.

To vary:
Use other fruits to fill the crêpes, e.g. apricots, pears or peaches and flavor the sauce with lemon, cherries, strawberries or other fruit, which can be heated in diluted redcurrant jelly. Flavor the sauce with cherry brandy.

To freeze:
The entire dish can be frozen then reheated gently just before serving. Freeze in a heatproof dish and heat in a slow oven. Use within 2 months.

To economize:
Serve as fruit-filled crêpes, top with hot marmalade and omit the sauce.

Lemon Syllabub

To make: 15 minutes   **No cooking   Serves 4–6**

¼ cup sugar cubes (see method)
2 large lemons
1¼ cups heavy cream
1¼ cups light cream
⅓ cup sweet white wine

Rub the sugar cubes over one of the lemons to absorb the flavor from the rind; if you have no sugar cubes and have to use sugar, then grate lemon into sugar. Cut 4–6 thin slices from the remaining lemon. Squeeze the juice from the whole lemon and any pieces remaining from the second lemon. Stir lemon juice into sugar until dissolved. Whip heavy cream, then gradually beat in the light cream, lemon juice and wine. Chill. Serve in small cups garnished with lemon twists, but do not freeze.

Cream Puff Pastry **To make:** 20 minutes   **To bake** (see method)   **Makes 12 large puffs or éclairs or 36 profiteroles**

⅔ cup water
2 tablespoons butter or margarine
pinch sugar or salt
¾ cup all-purpose flour
2 whole eggs and yolk of 1 egg or 3 small eggs

Put the water, butter or margarine and sugar (or salt if preparing puffs for a non-sweet filling) into a saucepan. Heat gently until the margarine or butter has melted. Remove from the heat and stir in the flour. Cook over low heat stirring all the time until the mixture is dry enough to form a ball and leave the pan clean. Once again remove the pan from the heat and beat in eggs, one at a time until smooth. Allow to cool then use as required.

Cream puffs: Grease and flour muffin pans and put in a spoonful of the mixture, or put in spoonfuls on greased and floured cookie sheets. To bake the puffs, allow about 10–15 minutes in a hot oven, 425°F., then lower the heat to 350–375°F. for a further 20 minutes. Split, remove any uncooked mixture, then return to a cool oven, 275°F. for a few minutes to dry out. Cool, and fill with sweetened whipped cream. Sprinkle with confectioners' sugar.

Eclairs: Put dough into a pastry bag with a ½-inch wide plain tip. Pipe into finger shapes or put into greased lady finger pans. Bake as Cream Puffs, above, but allow only 20 minutes baking time. Split when cooked, remove any uncooked mixture and "dry out" in a cool oven. Fill with sweetened whipped cream and top with chocolate icing, see below.

Profiteroles: Put small teaspoonfuls of the mixture on cookie sheets. Bake for only 15 minutes. Cool after baking, split and fill with sweetened whipped cream. Pile on a dish and top with the richer chocolate sauce on page 138.

Chocolate icing: Melt 4 oz. (4 squares) semisweet chocolate with 1 tablespoon vegetable shortening in a bowl set over hot water. Cool slightly then spread over the eclairs.

To freeze:
Baked cream puff pastry freezes well, but do not put on the chocolate icing before freezing. Use within 6–8 weeks.

Profiteroles

Apricot Meringue Cake

To make: 35 minutes **To bake:** 1 hour 20 minutes **Serves 8–10**

pound cake (see page 151)
1 can (1 lb. 12 oz.) apricots or 1 lb.
  cooked apricots
3 tablespoons apricot brandy
½ cup blanched almonds
For the meringue:
3 egg whites
¾ cup sugar
Quick tip:
See tips for making pound cake (Page 151).

Prepare pound cake and bake in two pans as page 151 then split each layer to give 4 thin layers. Drain the syrup from the canned or cooked apricots and blend 1 cup with the apricot brandy, slice the apricots and chop the almonds. Put the first layer of pound cake on a heatproof serving dish and moisten with ¼ of the apricot syrup, cover with sliced apricots and chopped almonds, then with the second layer of pound cake. Continue like this ending with fourth cake layer. Next, prepare the meringue. Spread over the top and sides of the cake. Put into a very slow oven, 225–250°F. and leave for 1 hour. Allow to cool.
To serve:
With cream or ice cream.
To freeze:
This cake is better frozen before topping with the meringue. Use within 3 months. Defrost then top with the meringue and continue as the recipe.

Lemon & Apricot Cheesecake

To make: 30 minutes **No cooking** **Serves 8–10**

For the crust:
8 oz. zwiebak or graham crackers
¼ cup butter
8 oz. drained cooked or canned
  apricot halves
For the filling:
2 eggs
¼ cup milk
¼ cup sugar
1½ cups cottage cheese
¼ cup lemon juice
3 tablespoons heavy cream
1 envelope unflavored gelatin
3 tablespoons water
To decorate:
8–9 candied cherries

Crush zwiebak or graham crackers with a rolling pin into fine crumbs, melt the butter and stir into the crumbs. Mix well, then press out into a greased 9-inch spring-form pan, coating the bottom and sides. Cover bottom with a layer of apricots, saving a few for decoration. Separate the egg yolks from the whites. Place the yolks, milk and sugar in a bowl or top part of a double boiler over hot but NOT BOILING water, and heat gently, stirring all the time until the mixture thickens enough to coat a spoon. Cool, then stir mixture into the sieved cottage cheese along with lemon juice and cream. Soften, then dissolve the gelatin in the water (see note below). Stir gelatin into the cheese mixture. Fold in the stiffly beaten egg whites. Pour the mixture into the lined pan, chill until firm. Decorate with reserved apricots and candied cherries.
To serve:
Remove sides from pan and serve cake on bottom of pan.
To vary:
Use fresh strawberries or other fruit instead of apricots.
To freeze:
This freezes perfectly. Use with 6–8 weeks.
  Note: It is easier to dissolve gelatin if it is first softened in cold liquid. Stir over low heat until gelatin is dissolved.

Ice Cream

To make: 15 minutes plus freezing **To cook:** 10–15 minutes **Serves 6**

2 eggs
⅓ cup confectioners' sugar
¼–½ teaspoon vanilla
1¼ cups milk
⅔ cup heavy cream
⅔ cup light cream
Quick tip:
Simply beat the heavy and light cream, add a little less sugar and flavoring and freeze.

Separate egg yolks from the whites. Make a custard with the yolks, sugar, vanilla and milk as page 145. Allow this to cool. Whip the heavy cream until it stands up in peaks, gradually beat in the light cream then fold into the custard. Pour into shallow dish.
To freeze:
Freeze until mushy; scrape from the dish into a bowl, beat lightly then fold in the stiffly beaten egg whites. Replace in dish and freeze until firm. Wrap in foil before storing. Use within 3 months.
To vary:
Flavor the custard with ¼ cup sifted cocoa or 1–2 teaspoons instant coffee. Stir in 1 cup thick fruit purée (strawberries, peaches, apricots, bananas, cherries). In this case, use all heavy cream.
To economize:
Use whipped evaporated milk instead of cream.

Crêpes Suzette

Crêpes Suzette

To make: 30 minutes   **To cook:** 20 minutes   **Serves 6**

For the crêpe batter:
1 cup all-purpose flour
pinch salt
2 eggs
1¼ cups milk
1 tablespoon oil or melted butter
To fry:
oil or butter
For the sauce:
½ cup superfine sugar
finely grated rind of 1 orange
juice of 2 oranges
1 tablespoon Grand Marnier or
   Curaçao
¼ cup brandy
To decorate:
orange slice
Quick tip:
Make batter in a blender.
To economize:
Omit liqueur and brandy.

Sift the flour and salt into a bowl. Add the eggs, then gradually beat in the milk to make a smooth batter. Finally stir in the oil or butter; the batter should be the consistency of heavy cream. Pour into a pitcher, beat before using. Pour a little oil into a 6-inch frying pan and heat until really hot, or melt a piece of butter. Pour off excess oil or butter. Pour in enough batter, about 3 tablespoons, to thinly coat the bottom of the pan, tilting and rotating the pan quickly so that the bottom is evenly covered. Cook until the underside is golden brown, turn and cook the other side. Slip the crêpe on oiled foil to cool. Repeat this method using the remaining batter to make 12 crêpes, stacking them as they are made. Heat the pan between each crêpe. Fold the crêpes into quarters and heat in the sauce. To make the sauce, stir the sugar in the frying pan until pale golden, then stir in the orange rind and juice. When all the crêpes have been heated, place on hot serving plates and keep warm. Stir the liqueur and brandy into the sauce remaining in the pan. Heat for 1 minute, ignite and pour while flaming over the crêpes.

To serve:
Immediately after cooking. This is a good dish to complete at the table. Decorate with a slice of orange, if wished.
To vary:
Fill the crêpes with redcurrant jelly before heating in the sauce.
   Use tangerine rind and juice instead of orange.
To freeze:
Prepare crêpes and freeze or prepare complete dish except for adding liqueur and brandy. Freeze and use within 3 months. Reheat in a pan over a very low heat, then add the liqueur or heat in a slow oven then add the liqueur.

137

Steamed Puddings

These puddings are ideal for chilly days, and are very easy to make. Remember to put a sponge or suet pudding in a steamer over boiling water and to cook fairly quickly for the first hour: this makes sure the pudding rises well and is light in texture. The cabinet pudding however is based upon an egg custard and must be cooked slowly.

Cake pudding:
Make the pound cake as page 151 (you can economize by using only ¼ cup margarine and sugar and mixing with 1 egg and milk). Put into a well-greased 1-quart heatproof bowl, cover with greased foil and steam for 1¼ hours. Serve a plain pound cake with warmed jam; an orange pound cake with hot marmalade; a chocolate pound cake with chocolate sauce, below; or put ¼-inch layer of honey in the bowl, top with the pound cake, then cook. Serve with honey flavored with lemon juice.
Freeze as Cherry Layer Pudding, opposite.

Chocolate Sauce

To make: 5 minutes   **To cook:** 10 minutes   **Serves 4**

1½ teaspoons cornstarch
1½ teaspoons cocoa
1¼ cups milk
1 tablespoon sugar
few drops vanilla
2 tablespoons butter

Mix the cornstarch and cocoa with a little cold milk. Heat the remainder of the milk, and when boiling beat into the blended mixture. Return to the heat and cook for 2–3 minutes, stirring constantly. Stir in sugar, vanilla and the butter, serve hot.
To vary:
If serving this sauce cold, use slightly more milk, stir as the sauce cools or put into the blender and whirl until smooth.
   A richer chocolate sauce is made by heating 4 oz. (4 squares) semisweet chocolate with ⅓ cup water, 2 tablespoons butter and 1 tablespoon corn syrup in a bowl set over hot water.

Cabinet Pudding

To make: 20 minutes   **To steam:** 1½ hours   **Serves 4–6**

2 cups sponge cake or ladyfingers
3 eggs or 3 egg yolks
¼ cup sugar
2½ cups milk
½ cup candied cherries
small piece angelica
⅓ cup blanched almonds

Make crumbs from the sponge cake or lady fingers. Beat the eggs with the sugar. Beat in warmed milk and pour onto the crumbs. Add the quartered cherries, finely diced angelica and chopped nuts. Stir well. Put into a well greased 1-quart heatproof bowl covered with greased foil. Steam over hot, but not boiling water, until firm, about 1½ hours.
To serve:
Unmold and serve with cream or custard sauce, page 145.
To freeze:
This pudding does not freeze well.
To economize:
Use leftover stale cake for this recipe.

Fruit Pudding

To make: 25 minutes   **To steam:** 3 hours   **Serves 6**

suet crust pastry made with 2½ cups all-purpose flour, etc.
about 1½ lbs. plums, sliced apples or fruit in season
sugar to taste (see method)
little water (see method)

Make the suet crust pastry and line a greased 1-quart heatproof bowl, as the method on page 72. Mix diced fruit (pitted or cored) with sugar to taste. Spoon into bowl and add enough water to come half way up the fruit. Roll out the remaining pastry and make a "lid", seal, then cover with greased foil. Steam rapidly for about 3 hours.
To serve:
Unmold and serve with cream or custard sauce, page 145.
To freeze:
As Cherry Layer Pudding, see opposite.

Cherry layer pudding

Cherry Layer Pudding

To make: 20 minutes **To steam:** 3 hours or 1 hour **Serves 4–6**

1 tablespoon butter
⅓ cup firmly packed brown sugar
1½ cups self-rising flour or
 all-purpose flour and 1½ teaspoons
 baking powder
pinch salt
6 tablespoons ground suet
2 cans (1 lb. 5 oz. each) cherry pie
 filling
Quick tip:
Use a pressure cooker (see method) or
make 4–6 individual puddings and
steam for 45 minutes.

Heavily butter a 1-quart heatproof bowl and sprinkle with 3 tablespoons of the sugar. Mix the flour and baking powder, if using, with the remaining sugar, salt and suet and add enough cold water to make a soft dough. Divide into 4 pieces of graduating sizes. Roll out the pieces individually, the smallest to fit the bottom of the bowl, the largest to fit the top. Place the smallest piece in the bottom. Drain off most of the sauce from the cherries and reserve. Put the cherries and pastry in layers in the bowl finishing with the largest piece of pastry. Cover with greased foil. Steam over boiling water. Allow 1 hour with the water boiling briskly then lower the heat so the water bubbles slowly and cook for a further 2 hours. To cook in a pressure cooker: Bring 1 quart water to a boil. Place the bowl on the trivet in the cooker, fit on the lid. Turn the heat to high, wait until the steam escapes freely from the vent. Lower the heat and cook gently with the vent open and steaming gently, for 15 minutes. Raise the heat, close vent and bring to 5 lbs. pressure for 40 minutes. Reduce pressure at room temperature.
To serve:
Hot with reserved cherry sauce or with custard sauce.
To vary:
Use any other fruit pie filling.
To freeze:
Cook, cool, freeze and use within 3 months. Or prepare, freeze and store for 2 months. Thaw out before cooking.
To economize:
Use more economical fruit with a little water and sugar to taste.

Making Pastry

There are many recipes in this book for pastry of various kinds. Learn to handle pastry gently but firmly so you do not stretch it in rolling.

Quantity of pastry: When a recipe states 2 cups pastry it means pastry made with 2 cups all-purpose flour, etc., not the total weight.

Fruit flans: The flan may be filled with cooked, canned, frozen or raw fruit. If using cooked or canned fruit, drain carefully. If using frozen fruit allow to defrost lightly and drain. If using raw fruit make a syrup of 1¼ cups water boiled with ½ cup sugar and simply put the fresh strawberries, cherries or other fruit in the warm syrup for 2–3 minutes then drain. In this way the fruit absorbs the flavor of the syrup but does not become too soft. To fill an 8-inch flan allow 1–1¼ lbs. fruit. Make the fleur pastry as the recipe below, or use pie crust, see page 122, made with 1½ cups all-purpose flour, etc. Roll out and line the bottom and sides of a flan pan or flan ring on a cookie sheet.

Fruit flan

Baking "blind" (Preparing baked pie shells): Fill the pie shell or flan shell with beans or rice to keep the pastry from shrinking in baking. Bake approximately 20–25 minutes; use a moderately hot oven 400°F. for fleur pastry and a hot oven, 425°F. for pie crust, until golden brown. Remove the beans or rice after 15 minutes. Allow the pastry to cool and fill as desired, or arrange the cold fruit in shell, see above. Measure the syrup drained from fruit and to each ⅔ cup allow 1 teaspoon arrowroot or cornstarch. Mix with the liquid and boil until thickened and clear. Cool slightly then spoon over the fruit.

Fleur Pastry

To make: 15 minutes   **To bake:** 20–25 minutes   **Serves 6–8**

½ cup butter or margarine
¼ cup sugar
1 egg yolk
1½ cups all-purpose flour
little cold water

Cream the butter or margarine and sugar until soft and light. Beat in the egg yolk, add the sifted flour, and stir with a fork. Gradually stir in enough water to make a firm elastic dough. Use as required.

To vary:
Omit ¼ cup all-purpose flour and add ¼ cup chopped nuts. Use only 6 tablespoons butter or margarine.

Pecan Pie

To make: 25 minutes   **To bake:** 40–50 minutes   **Serves 6–8**

pie crust made with 1½ cups
  all-purpose flour
3 eggs
⅔ cup sugar
¼ teaspoon salt
⅓ cup melted butter
1 cup dark corn syrup
1 cup pecan halves
Quick tip:
Use 9 oz. frozen pastry or 11 oz. pie crust mix.

Roll out the pie crust and line a 9-inch pie plate. Flute an edge on pie crust. Beat eggs and stir in remaining ingredients. Pour mixture into pie shell. Bake in a moderately hot oven, 375°F. for 40–50 minutes or until firm.
To serve:
Hot or cold with cream.
To freeze:
Cool, then freeze.
To economize:
Use peanuts instead of pecans.

One Crust Fruit Pies

Blackberry & Apple Pie

pie crust made with 2 cups
    all-purpose flour (see page 122)
little flour or cornstarch (see method)
3–4 tablespoons sugar
1 lb. cooking apples
8 oz. blackberries
¼ teaspoon ground cinnamon
    (optional)
To decorate:
sugar (optional — see method)
Quick tip:
Use frozen pie crust mix and canned
pie filling.
To economize:
Choose inexpensive fruit when in
season.

Crumb crust:
Mix 2 cups crushed graham crackers or zweibak with ½ cup softened butter and ¼ cup sugar. Mix with the hands until crumbly. Press firmly and evenly into a 9-inch pie shell, lining the bottom and sides. Chill. Crushed cornflakes or other crisp breakfast cereals could be used instead of crackers.

The recipe below is a pie as it has pastry both above and below the fruit. When you want to make a pie in a pie pan with one crust on top use pastry made with 1½ cups all-purpose flour. Put the fruit with sugar to taste and very little water into a pie pan. Roll out the pastry, cut a narrow strip and press this on to the rim of the pan. Roll out the remaining pastry to a piece large enough to cover the fruit. Moisten the pastry strip with water, lay the rolled out pastry over the top, trim, seal and flute the edges. Bake as below.

To make: 25 minutes   **To bake:** 30–40 minutes   **Serves 4–6**

Roll out half the pastry into a round and line an 8-inch pie plate. Sprinkle with a light dusting of flour or cornstarch and sugar; this absorbs the juice from the fruit and helps to keep the bottom pastry crisp. Peel, core and slice the apples. Wash and dry the blackberries. Place the apples and blackberries in the pie plate and sprinkle with the remaining sugar and the cinnamon, if wished. Brush the edge of the pastry with water. Roll out the remaining pastry to a round to fit the pie plate. Place on top of the fruit. Seal the edges, trim neatly, and decorate the edge. Make a hole in the center of the pastry with a skewer to allow the steam to escape. You can sprinkle the pastry with a little sugar before baking to give a glaze, if wished. Bake in a moderately hot to hot oven, 400–425°F. for 30–40 minutes, until the pastry is cooked and golden brown, lower the heat slightly after 20–30 minutes if the pastry is becoming too brown.
To serve:
Hot or cold with custard or cream.
To vary:
Use 1½ lbs. apples, strawberries, raspberries, pitted cherries or apricots in the pie.
    Sprinkle the bottom pastry with minute tapioca instead of flour.
To freeze:
This freezes well.

Lemon Meringue Pie

fleur pastry made with 1½ cups
    all-purpose flour (see opposite)
For the filling:
¼ cup cornstarch
1¼ cups cold water
2 tablespoons butter or margarine
grated rind and juice of 2 lemons
¾ cup sugar
2 eggs
Quick tip:
Use pie crust mix plus a little sugar or
frozen pie crust.

To make: 30 minutes   **To bake:** see method   **Serves 6–8**

Make the pastry and line an 8-inch flan ring or pie pan. Bake "blind", see opposite, until firm and golden; do not over-bake. Mix the cornstarch to a smooth paste with a little of the water. Bring the butter or margarine and remaining water to a boil, pour over the cornstarch mixture and stir well. Replace in saucepan and cook for 3 minutes, stirring all the time. Remove from the heat, stir in the lemon rind and juice and ½ cup of the sugar. Separate the yolks from the whites of the eggs. Stir the yolks into the lemon mixture. Cool and pour into the flan case or pie shell. Chill. Beat the egg whites until very stiff, beat in remaining ¼ cup sugar, 1 tablespoon at a time, or see below. Pile on top of the lemon mixture, making sure the meringue touches the edge of the pastry all around. Place in a slow oven, 275–300°F. for 20–30 minutes or until the meringue is lightly browned.
To serve:
Hot or cold. When serving cold prepare meringue as above, only fold in (do not beat) an extra ¼ cup sugar. Bake for 1 hour in a very slow oven, 225–250°F. This makes sure the meringue will not "shrivel" as it cools.
To vary:
Use orange rind and juice.
To freeze:
This freezes well, use within 6 weeks. Serve or heat gently as soon as defrosted.
To economize:
Use packaged lemon pudding and pie filling mix.

Apple pan dowdy

Apple Pan Dowdy

To make: 25 minutes   **To bake:** 45–50 minutes   **Serves 4**

3 good-sized cooking apples
1–2½ tablespoons firmly packed
   brown sugar
1–2½ tablespoons honey
grated nutmeg (see method)
ground cinnamon (see method)
1 cup self-rising flour or all-purpose
   flour and 1 level teaspoon baking
   powder
pinch salt
¼ cup sugar
1 egg
⅓ cup milk
¼ cup butter or margarine
little extra sugar
Quick tip:
Use canned apple pie filling plus the
spices.

Peel and slice the apples. Put into a greased 3 cup pie pan or shallow baking dish with the brown sugar, honey and a sprinkling of grated nutmeg and ground cinnamon. Do not add any water. Cover the dish with foil and bake in a moderate oven, 350°F. for about 15–20 minutes until the apples are nearly soft. Meanwhile make a thick batter mixture by blending the flour or flour and baking powder, salt, sugar, egg, milk and melted butter or margarine. Spoon the mixture over the apples, sprinkle lightly with extra sugar and bake for another 30–35 minutes. (If you use a deeper dish, allow about 45–50 minutes, lowering the heat after 25 minutes.)
To serve:
Turn the pudding upside-down on a dish, serve with cream, hard sauce or vanilla-flavored sauce.
To vary:
Use 3 cups pitted and quartered Italian prune plums in place of apples.
To freeze:
Cook, cool, freeze then wrap. Use within 2 months. Reheat gently from the frozen state.
To economize:
Use apples that are bruised and only half the butter or margarine.

142

Milk Puddings

The secret of a good milk pudding is slow cooking.

Use ⅓ cup regular rice (not converted) for each 2½ cups milk. Stir in ¼ cup sugar and pour into a buttered casserole. Drizzle 2 tablespoons melted butter or margarine over the top of the pudding. Bake in a slow oven, 275–300°F. for 1½–2 hours. Cream of wheat should be sprinkled on boiling milk in a pan, stirred over low heat until thickened, then transferred to a buttered casserole with sugar to taste and baked for about 45 minutes.

To freeze:
Milk puddings are better eaten freshly made. If you want to use a surplus of liquid milk, you can freeze this dish. Allow at least 24 hours to defrost and use within 3 months.

Apples with Calvados

To make: 10 minutes   **To cook:** 10 minutes   **Serves 4**

4 large Granny Smith or Rome Beauty apples
3 tablespoons butter
3 tablespoons vanilla sugar or sugar with ½ teaspoon vanilla
3 tablespoons Calvados (apple brandy)
Quick tip:
This is a very quick recipe.

Peel the apples, remove the cores and slice thinly. Melt the butter in a large frying pan, stir in the sugar, then add the apple slices. Sauté in the butter mixture until pale golden and transparent; when turning the apple slices, do so gently to avoid breaking them. Stir in vanilla (if using).

To serve:
When the apples are tender, warm the Calvados over heat in a soup ladle or spoon, ignite and pour over apples. Serve the apples as soon as the flames go out.

To vary:
Use sliced firm pears instead of apples.

To freeze:
Do not freeze this dish, but frozen apple slices could be used.

To economize:
Omit Calvados and flavor with orange juice.

Note: Vanilla sugar is sugar which is flavored with a vanilla bean. You can make it yourself by placing a cut vanilla bean in a jar of sugar, allow to stand one week before using.

Apples with Calvados

Caramelized Oranges

To make: 20 minutes   **To cook:** 15–20 minutes   **Serves 4**

4 large oranges
1¼ cups water
6 tablespoons sugar
Quick tip:
Prepare oranges as recipe then coat in warmed marmalade, diluted with a little water. Allow to cool.

Cut away the orange rind and white membrane but leave the fruit whole. Place in a serving dish. Slice the orange rind of 2 oranges into matchstick pieces. Simmer these in the water for 10 minutes. Take ¼ cup of this liquid and add to the sugar in a heavy pan. Stir until the sugar has dissolved, then boil until a golden caramel. Stir in cooked orange rind and ½ cup of the liquid in which it was cooked. Pour over the oranges.
To serve:
Chill and serve with cream or ice cream.
To freeze:
Oranges can be frozen, but not caramel, so this is essentially a dessert to serve when freshly made.

Apple Lemon Mold

To make: 20 minutes plus setting   **No cooking**   **Serves 4**

grated rind and juice of 2 lemons
2½ cups hot thick applesauce
1 envelope unflavored gelatin
3 tablespoons honey
To decorate:
lemon
Quick tip:
Use canned apple sauce.

Stir the grated rind of the lemons into the hot applesauce. Mix the gelatin with the juice from the lemons. Stir into the hot applesauce with the honey. Pour into a 3 cup mold rinsed with cold water. Chill until firm.
To serve:
Unmold by dipping mold into lukewarm water for a few seconds and decorate with halved lemon slices.
To vary:
Use other fruit purée such as apricot, peach.
To freeze:
Either freeze the dish and use within 2–3 weeks, or use frozen purée.

Apple lemon mold

Egg Custards

An egg custard needs careful cooking, as excessive heat or cooking for too long a period means that the temperature of the milk and eggs will reach boiling point. The custard will then "curdle", i.e. separate, so it has an unpleasant layer of water.

For a soft custard sauce:
Beat 2 eggs or 2 egg yolks and 1–2 tablespoons sugar with 2½ cups warm milk. Flavor with a few drops of vanilla or a strip of lemon rind (but no lemon juice). Cook in the top of a double boiler or bowl over hot, but not boiling water, stirring all the time, until the mixture is thick enough to coat a wooden spoon; or use a heavy pan over very low heat. If serving cold, cover with foil to prevent a skin forming, or stir several times as the mixture cools.

For a baked custard:
Beat 4 eggs or egg yolks, with 1–2 tablespoons sugar and 2½ cups warm milk. If you intend to unmold the custard you can increase the yolks to 5. Strain into a 3-cup baking dish and either steam over hot water or bake in a slow oven, 275–300°F. Bake about 1 hour, depending upon the depth of the custard. To prevent the sides of the custard becoming hard and to lower the temperature, stand the dish containing the egg custard in a pan of cold water until cooled to room temperature. Chill.

To freeze:
A baked egg custard does not freeze well unless using half heavy cream and half milk, but an unbaked egg custard can be frozen, so if you have made the custard and then find it will not be eaten, freeze it before baking rather than waste it. Use within 2 months and bake from the frozen state.

Puddings Based on Egg Custard

These puddings are made and baked as egg custards, although, since the proportion of milk, etc., varies the cooking times may not be exactly the same. See also Cabinet Pudding, page 138. All recipes serve 4.

Bread and butter pudding:
Cut thin slices of white bread and spread with butter. Cut into squares or triangles and put into a pie dish with ⅓ cup chopped dried fruit. Prepare a custard with 2 eggs or yolks, 2 cups milk, and 1–2 tablespoons sugar. Pour mixture over the bread and butter. Sprinkle a little extra sugar on top together with grated nutmeg. Bake as the baked custard above, although you can raise the oven temperature slightly to crisp the bread on top.

Caramel custard:
Make a caramel sauce. Stir 6 tablespoons sugar and ¼ cup water over low heat until the sugar has dissolved. Continue cooking without stirring, until a golden brown caramel. Add 2 tablespoons water and stir until blended. Cool slightly then pour the caramel into a 3-cup baking dish, turning the dish around, so the sauce coats the sides and bottom. Cool. Prepare a baked custard mixture with 4 eggs or 4–5 yolks, etc. Strain into the dish and bake as for baked custard. Leave until nearly cold, then chill to serve, loosen edges then unmold on a serving dish.

Queen of puddings:
Spread a little jam over the bottom of a pie pan. Put 1 cup fine pound cake or vanilla wafer crumbs into a bowl. Beat 2 egg yolks with 1–2 tablespoons sugar. Beat in 1¼–2 cups milk and strain over the crumbs. Mix thoroughly, pour into the pie dish. Bake as for baked custard. Remove from the oven, spread the pudding with more jam. Beat the egg whites until stiff, beat in ¼ cup sugar, 1 tablespoon at a time. Spread the meringue mixture over the top of the pudding, return to the oven and bake for 15 minutes or until cooked. Serve this pudding hot.

Jelly roll pudding:
As Queen of Puddings above but omit the jam. Use ½-inch thick slices of jelly roll to line pie pan. Prepare custard as for Queen of Puddings. Pour into pan. Bake as Queen of Puddings then remove from the oven, top with meringue and continue baking as Queen of Puddings.

Baking for the Family

Home made bread and cakes enable you to add rich flavor and nutrition to your table.

When baking remember: Check oven temperatures with a thermometer from time to time to make sure your oven is heating properly. Careful measuring, mixing and baking are part of the secret of successful results.

Follow the recommended method of mixing the ingredients, in a Pound cake (page 151), for example, you are advised to "fold" in the flour, this retains the light texture.

Careful measuring is important. Level measurements in standard cups and spoons that are correct for measuring dry and liquid ingredients.

To freeze: Many cakes and breads freeze well, see under the individual recipes for details. When a cake is iced or decorated, freeze without covering, then wrap when frozen hard.

Economical baking: Yeast baking is one of the most economical methods of providing bread etc. for the family, recipes and suggestions are on the right and pages 148 and 149.

Yeast baking: Baking with yeast is not only very simple, but very economical too, as you can produce a whole batch of bread and rolls at little expense. The quantity of dough given in the bread recipe on page 148 will prepare three out of the four loaves suggested below or some of the other recipes on page 149.

All-purpose flour is used for making bread, but if you can obtain bread flour, you will have an even better result.

To make loaves: You will find the recipe for a white bread dough, with variations on this basic recipe on page 148.

The quantity given in this recipe is enough to make three loaves of bread. The same basic bread recipe can be used to make rolls or buns and you will find the instructions for shaping and baking these on page 149. Make the bread dough, allow this to rise until double, then knead well, cut the dough into three parts and proceed as below.

Round loaf: Shape the dough into a smooth round. Either put on a greased cookie sheet or into a 6-inch round cake pan. Cover the pan lightly and allow to rise for about 1 hour or until double in bulk in a warm place. Bake for 35–40 minutes (about 20 minutes in a moderately hot to hot oven 400–425°F.) then reduce temperature to moderate, 350°F.) To test if the bread is cooked, thump the loaf and it should sound hollow.

Regular loaf: Shape dough into a roll 8 inches long and place into a greased 9 × 5 × 3-inch pan. Let rise and bake as for round loaf.

Fruit loaf: Knead ½ cup chopped dried fruit into one batch of dough. Roll lightly into an oblong 9 × 12 inches. Fold in three shaping an oblong 9 × 4 inches then put into the greased 9 × 5 × 3-inch loaf pan. Brush with egg beaten with water; let rise and bake as for round loaf.

Poppy seed loaf: Roll with hand into a long strip, fold in half and twist the two ends loosely, brush with egg beaten with water and sprinkle with poppy seeds. Let rise as for round loaf, but bake for about 30 minutes.

Scones or Biscuits

To make: 5–6 minutes **To bake:** 7–10 minutes **Makes 12**

2 cups all-purpose flour
½ teaspoon salt
½ teaspoon baking soda
1 teaspoon cream of tartar
3 tablespoons butter or margarine
2 tablespoons sugar (optional)
⅔ cup milk
Quick tip:
All scones are quick to make and bake.

Sift the flour, salt, baking soda and cream of tartar into a bowl. Rub the butter or margarine into the flour with the tips of your fingers; add the sugar if desired. Stir in the milk to give a soft, but not too wet, consistency. Lightly flour a working surface and knead dough a few times until smooth. Pat or roll out the dough until it is ½-inch thick. Either cut into squares or cut into 2-inch rounds, using a biscuit cutter or top of a small glass. Place the scones on a cooking sheet and bake in hot oven, 425°F. for 10 minutes or until puffed and golden brown.

To serve:
When hot with butter and jam.

To vary:
Use self-rising flour and omit the baking soda and cream of tartar. If desired add only half the quantities for a very light scone.
    Brown scones: Use half white and half wholewheat flour.
    Cheese scones: Omit sugar, season flour with salt, use only 2 tablespoons butter or margarine and ½ cup grated cheese.
    Fruit scones: Add ⅓ cup chopped dried fruit or raisins.
    Oatmeal scones: Use half quick-cooking oatmeal and half flour.
    Potato scones: Use half flour and half thick mashed potatoes.
    Molasses scones: Omit sugar and add 1 tablespoon molasses to the dough before stirring in milk.

To freeze:
Scones freeze perfectly. Bake, cool and freeze, then use within 6 months. Heat gently for a short time from the frozen state.
    If preferred, freeze on cookie sheets before baking, then pack, use within 2 months. Thaw out before baking.

To economize:
Halve the butter or margarine.

White Bread

To make: 30 minutes plus rising **To bake:** see page 146 **Makes 3 loaves**
9 × 5 × 3-inch pans

1 envelope active dry yeast
3¾ cups warm water, milk or milk and water
2 teaspoons sugar (see method)
12 cups all-purpose flour
1 tablespoon salt
½ cup lard or margarine
Quick tip:
Make the dough into rolls (see opposite).

Mix yeast with the warm liquid and the sugar. Wait for about 10 minutes. Mix the flour and salt, cut in the lard or margarine, add the yeast liquid. Mix together until you have a firm dough and the bowl is clean. Turn out on a floured surface and knead until a smooth elastic dough. To tell if the dough is well kneaded, press with a lightly floured finger; if the impression comes out, the dough has been handled enough. Either return to the bowl and cover with a cloth or put into a large, lightly oiled plastic bag and tie loosely at the top. Allow the dough to rise until double its original size. You can control the time quite appreciably; if you are in a hurry, leave in a warm, but not too hot, place for 1–1½ hours or about 2 hours at room temperature; or 12–24 hours in a refrigerator. Allow to return to room temperature then shape, let rise and bake as page 146.

To vary:
Wholewheat bread: Use half white and half stoneground (wholewheat) flour. You may have to add more liquid.

To freeze:
Use 50% more yeast, let rise as above, then form into desired shape. Place shapes into large, lightly oiled plastic bags and seal. Freeze but use within 8 weeks. Always allow to return to room temperature and rise until double the bulk before shaping. Baked bread can be kept for 6 weeks. Wrap and warm in the oven or thaw out at room temperature.

To economize:
Use water to mix the dough. Never waste left-over bread, the crumbs can be used in cooking. If you brush the crust of the loaf with water or milk, it does not harden with reheating. You can crisp up quite stale bread by heating it in a moderate oven for about 20 minutes. If you dislike a crisp outside crust, wrap the moistened bread in foil before warming through.

Swedish Tea Ring

Yeast breads

Punch down risen White Bread dough and knead again. Cut off ⅓ of the dough. On a floured surface roll out to a 12 × 9-inch rectangle. Brush with 2 tablespoons melted butter, sprinkle with ⅓ cup firmly packed brown sugar, a little cinnamon and ½ cup finely chopped blanched almonds. Roll up like a jelly roll, form into a round and seal the ends. Put on a greased cookie sheet. Make cuts with scissors, cutting not quite all the way through about 1-inch apart. Turn slices on side showing cut surface. Allow to rise and bake as the round loaf, page 146. When cold top with icing made with ½ cup confectioners' sugar, blended with a little warm water. Decorate with blanched almonds and halved candied cherries.

To Make Rolls

Note: In shaping rolls remember the baked size will be 3 times as big as the unbaked size. Shape rolls, place on cookie sheet, let rise until double and then bake at 375°F. for 12–15 minutes or until brown.

Finger rolls:
Form dough into finger shapes. Place on greased cookie sheets. Brush with egg beaten with water.

Knot rolls:
Roll the dough into a 7-inch long strip. Tie in a loose knot. Place the rolls on greased cookie sheet. Brush with egg beaten with water. Sprinkle with poppy seeds.

Buns:
These are large, fairly flat rolls, ideal for serving with Hamburgers, see page 77. Make the dough a little softer than usual, roll to ½ inch thickness, cut into 4-inch rounds then flatten slightly when on cookie sheets before rising. Brush with egg beaten with water.

149

Making Cakes

There are several ways of mixing cakes. Melting some of the ingredients is both quick and simple, see opposite and page 152. Another easy method is to cut the fat into the flour, but do not over-handle the mixture when mixing by this method. The creaming method of mixing is described below and on page 151, and beaten sponges on page 153.

Always choose the type of flour recommended in the recipe, as this is very important.

Test a cake thoroughly before turning it out of the pan. Most cakes are baked until they are firm to the touch, but see the individual recipes.

Secrets of Light Cakes

Most light cakes are made by creaming; this method is used in the well known recipes below and on other pages in this section. Always cream (i.e. beat), the fat and sugar well. This is important whether you use an electric mixer or beat with a wooden spoon. The reason for creaming is to incorporate as much air as possible and so lighten the cake; modern soft margarines cream easily. Use superfine sugar for light cakes as this has a finer texture than granulated. Do not add the eggs too quickly, as the mixture could "curdle" (separate) and this spoils the smooth texture. If the mixture shows any signs of "curdling" add a little flour at once and stir gently and carefully into the mixture to retain the lightness of the cake.

Cider streusel cake

Cider Streusel Cake

To make: 15 minutes   **To bake:** 50 minutes   **Serves 8–10**

4½ cups self-rising flour or
    all-purpose flour and 4½ teaspoons
    baking powder
⅔ cup firmly packed brown sugar
½ cup pitted dates
¼ cup molasses
1¼ cups cider or apple juice
2 eggs
For the topping:
3 tablespoons sugar
6 tablespoons all-purpose or
    self-rising flour
3 tablespoons butter
6 tablespoons walnuts
½ teaspoon ground cinnamon
¼ cup apricot or grape jam

Sift the flour or flour and baking powder. Add the sugar and chopped dates. Heat molasses and cider until warm, then stir into the flour mixture. Lastly add the eggs and mix thoroughly. Line a 9-inch square cake pan with greased foil leaving a 1-inch overhang, and pour in the mixture. Bake in a very moderate oven, 325°F. for 30 minutes. Meanwhile prepare the topping, mix the sugar and flour, cut in the butter, stir in the chopped walnuts and cinnamon until crumbly. Remove the cake from the oven, spread with the jam carefully and press the crumbs over the top. Return to the oven for a further 20 minutes. As one cannot press this cake to see if it is firm to the touch, test to see if it is cooked by inserting a toothpick, if it comes out clean the cake is baked. Cool in the pan for 10–15 minutes, pull out using foil.

To serve:
Although the cake itself has no fat in it, it is better if aged for 2 days before cutting.

Pound Cake

To make: 10–15 minutes   **To bake:** 30–40 minutes   **Serves 4–5**

1 cup margarine, butter or vegetable
    shortening
1 cup superfine sugar
2 eggs
1 cup self-rising flour or all-purpose
    flour and 1 teaspoon baking
    powder
Quick tip:
Use your mixer for creaming the fat and sugar and adding the eggs. Fold in the flour by hand. Use soft margarine, put all the ingredients into the bowl and beat. This cake is not as light, but is very acceptable.

Cream the margarine, butter or fat with the sugar until soft and light in color, using a wooden spoon. If using the mixer warm the bowl, but not the fat, to ease mixing. Gradually beat in the eggs, then fold in the sifted flour or flour and baking powder. Divide the mixture between two 8-inch greased and floured layer cake pans. Bake in a slow oven, 325°F. for 30–40 minutes until just firm to the touch. Cool for 2–3 minutes in the pans, unmold carefully and cool on racks.

To serve:
Fill with jam or jam and whipped cream and sprinkle top with confectioners' sugar or superfine sugar and serve with coffee, or for tea. Or, fill with fruit and cream and serve as a dessert.

To vary:
Chocolate pound cake: Omit 2 tablespoons flour and use cocoa instead.
    Orange pound cake: Add finely grated rind of 1–2 oranges to margarine and sugar. Use small eggs and add orange juice to give the correct consistency. Lemon rind and juice could also be used.

To freeze:
Use within 10 weeks, and allow 3–4 hours to defrost.

To economize:
Use only ¼ cup fat and ¼ cup sugar, one egg and milk to mix to the correct consistency.

Dundee Cake

To make: 15–20 minutes   **To bake:** 2–2¼ hours   **Serves 8–10**

¾ cup margarine or butter
¾ cup superfine sugar
3 large eggs
2 cups all-purpose flour
1½ teaspoons baking powder
1 lb. chopped mixed dried fruit
⅓ cup candied cherries
⅓ cup chopped candied peel
little milk, about ⅓ cup
To decorate:
⅓ cup blanched sliced almonds
Quick tip:
Use your mixer for creaming the fat and sugar and adding the eggs or use a soft margarine (see Pound Cake above).

Cream the margarine or butter and sugar together and gradually beat in the eggs. Fold in the sifted flour and baking powder, then fruit, cherries and peel and just enough milk to make a soft, creamy consistency like a pound cake batter. Put dough into an 8-inch greased and floured, or lined with wax paper and greased, spring-form pan and sprinkle with the sliced almonds. Brush these with a little egg white (there is enough left in the egg shells after making the cake). Bake for 2–2¼ hours in a very moderate oven, 325°F., reducing the heat to slow (300°F.) after about 1–1½ hours. Cool slightly, unmold carefully.

To vary:
Spiced Dundee cake: Sift 1–2 teaspoons apple pie spice with the flour.

To freeze:
It is generally pointless to freeze a rich Dundee cake, as this matures and keeps well in a tin for up to two months. If you want to keep it longer, freeze and use within 2–3 months.

To economize:
Use only ⅔ cup butter, ⅔ cup sugar and 2 eggs. Increase the amount of baking powder to 2 teaspoons with all-purpose flour or use self-rising flour and increase the milk to give a soft, creamy consistency.

Golden Ginger Loaf

To make: 15 minutes   **To bake:** 1–1¼ hours   **Serves 10–12**

2½ cups all-purpose flour
1 teaspoon baking soda
½ teaspoon ground ginger
¾ cup honey
½ cup vegetable shortening
¾ cup sugar
3 tablespoons syrup from a jar of
    preserved ginger
2 tablespoons milk
2 eggs

To decorate:
1 tablespoon honey
few leaves candied angelica
3–4 tablespoons preserved ginger

Quick tip:
The melting method of mixing is one
of the speediest ways of preparing a
cake.

Sift the dry ingredients into the mixing bowl. In a saucepan mix honey, fat and sugar. Heat gently until the fat melts, then pour over the flour and beat well. Warm the syrup and milk in a pan, add to the flour mixture with the eggs and beat until smooth. Line a 9 × 5 × 3-inch loaf pan with greased foil. Pour in the mixture. Bake in a very moderate oven, 300–325°F. for 1–1¼ hours until just firm to the touch, do not over-bake. Remove from the oven and cool in the pan for about 15 minutes. Remove from the pan, take off the foil, then brush the top with the honey and press the pieces of angelica and sliced ginger into position.

To serve:
Plain or spread with butter, with coffee or tea. This is also delicious sliced and topped with applesauce.

To vary:
To make a darker, stronger flavored loaf, use molasses in place of honey. The amount of ground ginger may be increased to 2 teaspoons as this recipe gives a very mild flavor.

To freeze:
This freezes excellently. Use within 3 months.

To economize:
Omit preserved ginger and increase the milk to ⅓ cup and the ground ginger to 1½ teaspoons.

Golden ginger loaf

Raisin loaf cake

Raisin Loaf Cake

To make: 15 minutes (see method)   **To bake:** 1¾–2 hours   **Serves 10–12**

3 cups all-purpose flour
1 teaspoon pumpkin pie spice
1½ teaspoons baking soda
¾ cup butter or margarine
1 tablespoon lemon juice
1¼ cups + 1 tablespoon milk
1 cup firmly packed brown sugar
1 cup currants
½ cup raisins
Quick tip:
This is a quick cake to prepare.

Line a 9 × 5 × 3-inch loaf pan with greased foil. Sift the flour, spice and baking soda into a bowl. Cut the butter or margarine into the flour until the mixture resembles fine breadcrumbs. Add the lemon juice to the milk (the milk will sour). Mix the sugar, currants and raisins with the dry ingredients. Gradually add the sour milk, stirring until smooth. Leave the mixture covered at room temperature for several hours or overnight. Spoon the mixture into the prepared pan. Bake in a very moderate oven, 325°F. for 1¾–2 hours, or until firm to the touch. Leave for a few minutes in the pan before unmolding on a wire rack to cool. Remove the foil. Wrap in foil when cold and store in an airtight container for not longer than a week.
To freeze:
This is the type of fruit cake to bake then freeze, as the storage life is limited in a tin. Use within 2 months.
To economize:
This is an economical cake, but use vinegar in place of lemon juice.

Muffins

To make: 10 minutes   **To bake:** 20–25 minutes   **Makes 10–12**

2 cups self-rising flour or all-purpose
   flour and 2 teaspoons baking
   powder
½ teaspoon salt
¼ cup margarine
¼ cup sugar
½ cup chopped dried fruit
1 egg
1 cup milk

Sift the flour, or flour and baking powder and salt. Cut in the margarine, add sugar, the fruit, then the beaten egg and milk. Stir until just mixed. Dough will be lumpy. Spoon mixture into greased muffin pan. Sprinkle lightly with additional sugar and bake for 20–25 minutes in a hot oven, 400°F.
To vary:
Flavor the muffins with grated lemon or orange rind and mix with fruit juice instead of milk.
   Coconut and fruit muffins: Use 1½ cups all-purpose flour and ½ cup flaked coconut.
To freeze:
These economical cakes will not become stale if you freeze them the day they are baked. Use within 3 months.

Yellow Cake

To make: 10–15 minutes   **To bake:** 40 minutes   **Serves 10**

¾ cup butter or margarine
¾ cup sugar
2 cups self-rising flour or all-purpose
   flour and 2 teaspoons baking
   powder
½ teaspoon salt
3 eggs
1 teaspoon grated lemon rind
¾ cup milk
little extra sugar
⅓ cup chopped candied lemon peel
Quick tip:
Use the mixer to cream the butter and sugar and add the eggs, or use soft margarine (see Pound Cake page 151).

Cream the butter or margarine and sugar together until soft and light. Sift the flour or flour and baking powder and salt. Beat the eggs. Stir the eggs into butter mixture with lemon rind. Add flour and milk alternately beating after each addition. Put into a greased and floured 9 × 13 × 2-inch cake pan. Sprinkle with a little sugar and top with the peel. Bake for 40 minutes in a moderate oven, 350°F.
To vary:
Cherry cake: Ingredients and method of mixing as above. Fold in 1 cup halved candied cherries which should be rinsed in cold water, dried and floured before adding to the mixture.
   Seed cake: Add 2–3 teaspoons caraway seeds or poppy seeds to the batter before baking.
To freeze:
This freezes well; use within 10 weeks. Allow 4–5 hours to defrost.

Index

155